CURRY BIBLE

CURRY BIBLE

EXOTIC AND FRAGRANT CURRIES
FROM AROUND THE WORLD

MRIDULA BALJEKAR

Love Food ® is an imprint of Parragon Books Ltd

Parragon
Queen Street House
4 Queen Street
Bath BA1 1HE, UK

Copyright © Parragon Books Ltd 2008

Love Food ® and the accompanying heart device is a trademark of Parragon Books Ltd

ISBN: 978-1-4054-9569-1

Printed in China

Contributing author: Mridula Baljekar
Additional recipes by Beverly LeBlanc, Judy Williams, and Corinne Trang
Photography by Mike Cooper
Food styling by Sumi Glass, Carole Handslip, and Lincoln Jefferson
Cover design by Talking Design
Internal design by Sarah Edwards

Notes for the Reader
This book uses imperial, metric, and US cup measurements. Follow the same units of measurement throughout; do not mix imperial and metric. All spoon measurements are level: teaspoons are assumed to be 5 ml, and tablespoons are assumed to be 15 ml. Unless otherwise stated, milk is assumed to be whole, eggs and individual vegetables such as potatoes are medium, and pepper is freshly ground black pepper.

The times given are an approximate guide only. Preparation times differ according to the techniques used by different people and the cooking times may also vary from those given as a result of the type of oven used. Optional ingredients, variations or serving suggestions have not been included in the calculations.

Recipes using raw or very lightly cooked eggs should be avoided by infants, the elderly, pregnant women, convalescents, and anyone with a chronic condition. Pregnant and breastfeeding women are advised to avoid eating peanuts and peanut products. Sufferers from nut allergies should be aware that some of the ready-prepared ingredients used in the recipes in this book may contain nuts. Always check the packaging before use.

Contents

Introduction

Curries are popular the world over because of the exciting colors, varied textures, and complex flavors produced by the spices. Some of the world's most exotic curries are found in India and Southeast Asia. These regions offer delectable curries with distinctly different cooking styles, which are directly influenced by internal and external factors prevalent in each country. The cuisines of the subcontinent of India and the Southeast Asian countries, such as Burma, Malaysia, Indonesia, and Vietnam, have been influenced by the invasion of foreign powers and their subsequent rule. The mouthwatering curries eaten in these countries have tingled the taste buds of the world and curry has now become a firm favorite in almost every corner of the globe. But what exactly is a "curry"? There is more than one explanation of the meaning of the word: one source suggests that it originates from the South Indian language Tamil in which curry (spelt "kaari") means a spicy sauce. It is also believed that, during the British Raj, the spelling of "kaari" was changed to "curry." However, more recent research shows that the history of the curry can be traced back to the dawn of time. Archeological evidence found in Mesopotamia (present-day Iraq) mentions a meat dish with a spicy sauce that could have been the first recorded curry. Today, however, there is no doubt that the word "curry" has become synonymous with a spicy sauce in which meat, poultry, fish, or vegetables are cooked.

The first record of India's spice wealth goes back to as early as AD 629, when the Chinese traveler Huien Tsang passed through India. It was indeed the lure of spices that attracted a host of foreign invaders to India. Nomadic tribes, traders, and pilgrims entered India and their cooking styles became a part of the colorful cuisine of the country.

The geographical position of Southeast Asia, on the far side of India's holy river, the Ganges, has been described as Farther India. The diverse climatic and geographical conditions of this region have given rise to a wide range of crops resulting in a diverse cuisine. A breathtaking range of food, with very clear regional differences, makes Asian cuisine a multidimensional tapestry that is as rich as it is colorful and as intoxicating as it is inimitable. It reflects the heritage of the people of its land and the influences of historical and cultural developments and religious beliefs.

Asian curries, especially Indian, today have gained global recognition. The diverse nature of the curries of Asia has been extended further in other countries around the world because of the need to combine spices with locally grown ingredients. In recent years the appeal of spices has grown at an astonishing rate throughout the world. The exquisite flavors of high-quality spices grown in India have added a new dimension to international cuisine. Today India is rightly described as the "spice bowl of the world."

The Spice Route

Spices have been used for thousands of years in Asia, Arabia, and the Mediterranean. In 332 BC, Alexander the Great founded Alexandria, which soon became the meeting point for spice merchants from East and West.

The Greeks used several routes to bring spices from the East. History has it that the oldest route started from the Malabar Coast in southern India. This route then went around the coast of Arabia and up the Red Sea into the Mediterranean region. It became the main trade route between Asia and Europe for many years. At the same time, an overland trading route, running from Europe through Asia Minor into Asia and leading right up to China, was often used by merchants for trading in silk and spices.

When initially the Portuguese, and finally the British, established their empires in India, they acquired control of the Asian maritime routes. This diminished the importance of the "Spice Route," but spices still played a far-reaching and influential role in the economies of many countries.

India and Southeast Asia have had the magical and mysterious power to attract visitors and traders since ancient times. The Arabs, British, Dutch, Portuguese, and Spanish came to India and Southeast Asia, lured by spices. Afghanistan on the northern border of India and the paradise islands of Indonesia in the south have enticed foreign traders over the centuries.

Spices lie at the heart of the strong resemblance in the cooking styles of India and Southeast Asia. It is also the spices that set apart the culinary styles of these regions. For instance, the cuisine of south India, with its use of coconut and curry leaves, is strikingly similar to that of Southeast Asia, where coconut is used extensively with kaffir lime leaves and lemongrass to add extra zest. In Malaysian cuisine one sees a strong Indian influence contributed by the commercial community of India who migrated to this region several centuries ago. The evidence of European influences in the cuisine of Vietnam and the

islands of the Philippines is strong even today. Vietnamese cuisine draws influences from the French, while the Philippines show a strong tendency toward Spanish cooking styles. Thailand, on the other hand, boasts a totally indigenous style of cooking as the country has been free from colonization.

The influence of spices in the West has reached an astonishing level in recent years. As well as in kitchens and homes, spicy food is also finding its way to the supermarket shelves in Europe, the United States, Canada, Australia, Africa, and many other countries. International trade in spices has enjoyed phenomenal growth in recent years and well over 500,000 tons, exceeding a value of $1,500 million, is exported globally by India.

A recent publication shows that the first "curry house" opened in Britain in 1809. Today there are 9,000 Indian restaurants in Britain and numerous Southeast Asian restaurants are enjoying huge popularity. This trend has traveled across the Atlantic and many people in parts of the United States and Canada are now enjoying curries in restaurants and in the form of prepared meals from supermarkets. Making an authentic curry at home has become easier than ever because Asian ingredients are readily available from supermarkets and gourmet stores. The exotic curries of Asia have become the choice for dinner parties because they provide interest and excitement with their exquisite tastes, flavors, and appetizing appearances. It is evident that the curry craze will continue to grow and the spices of Asia will continue to inspire palates worldwide.

Essential curry ingredients

Aniseed

Anise is native to India and looks rather like celery seed. It is related to caraway and cumin, but the flavor is more akin to that of thyme. Anise aids digestion.

Asafetida

Obtained from the resinous gum of a tropical plant, asafetida can be bought from Asian stores in block or powder form. It should be used sparingly because of its strong flavor.

Bay leaf

Bay leaves used in curries are different from those used in the West. Asian bay leaves come from the cassia tree, whereas the Western ones are obtained from sweet bay laurel. Western bay leaves are a popular substitute, as the Asian ones are rarely available in the West.

Cardamom

Cardamom has been used in Asian cooking since ancient times. Whole cardamom pods are used to flavor rice and different types of sauces. Ground cardamom, used in many desserts and drinks, can be bought from most Asian stores, but grinding small quantities at home using a coffee mill will produce better flavors.

Chiles, fresh

Chiles come in different sizes, strengths, and colors. Generally, the small thin ones are hot while the large fleshy ones tend to be milder. Most of the heat is in the seeds and the membranes. It is best to remove them if you prefer a milder flavor.

Chili powder

When fresh green chiles are ripe, they turn a rich red. These are dried to obtain dried red chiles. Chili powder is made by finely grinding dried red chiles. Crushed dried chiles are also made by grinding dried red chiles to a coarse texture. These are sold in Asian stores.

Cinnamon

One of the oldest spices, cinnamon is obtained from the dried bark of a tropical plant related to the laurel family. It has a warm flavor and is used in both savory and sweet dishes.

Cloves

Cloves are the unripened dried buds of a southern Asian evergreen tree. They have a strong distinctive flavor and are used both whole and ground. Clove oil is used to relieve toothache.

Coconut

Coconut milk is made by grating, blending, and squeezing the juice from coconut flesh. The first extraction is thicker and the second, made from the remaining blended coconut by soaking it in water, is thinner. The second extraction can be boiled for a longer time than the first, which releases too much of the oil when boiled. Canned coconut milk is an ideal substitute for the second extraction.

Dry unsweetened coconut is grated fresh coconut that has been dried to prolong its shelf life. It is used in both sweet and savory dishes, including a variety of

Coconut cream is also made by combining coconut flesh with water, but with a higher ratio of coconut to water. It is therefore richer and thicker than coconut milk. Canned coconut cream is available from most supermarkets.

Dry unsweetened coconut is grated fresh coconut that has been dried to prolong its shelf life. It is used in both sweet and savory dishes, including a variety of desserts and sweetmeats. Coconut milk can be made by soaking dry unsweetened coconut in hot milk and blending it in an electric blender.

Coriander

The fruit produced by the mature cilantro plant is the seed that is used as a spice. Its sweet, mellow flavor is very important in Southeast Asian curries.

Cumin

Cumin is used either whole or ground. It has a warm and assertive taste. The whole seeds are used to flavor the oil for many vegetarian dishes and the ground version is used in curries. There are two varieties: black and white. Each has its own distinct flavor and one cannot be substituted for the other. Black cumin is sometimes confused with caraway.

Curry leaves

A hallmark of southern Indian cooking, these have an assertive flavor. Fresh and dried versions are sold in Asian stores. Dried ones can be stored in an airtight jar and the fresh ones can be frozen and used when required.

Curry powder and curry pastes

Curry powder is a British invention that was created in southern India and exported to Britain when the British returned home at the end of the Raj. It is produced by blending several spices together, making it easier to create curries. In India, spices are individually blended during cooking and curry powder is never used. It is, however, a popular ingredient in Southeast Asian curries.

Curry pastes are commonly used in Southeast Asian cooking and are made in the similar way to curry powder, but oil is added to the powdered spices in order to make the mixture into a paste. This also helps to preserve the wet spice blend. Wet spice blends, cooked out correctly, impart a superior flavor. The tradition of curry pastes perhaps originated from the traditional Indian and Southeast Asian practice of grinding spices in a grinding stone with water added to them.

Fennel seeds

These have a taste similar to that of anise. They have been used in curries since ancient times. In India, fennel is used as a breath freshener.

Fenugreek

A strong and aromatic herb, fenugreek is cultivated in India and Pakistan, but is native to the Mediterranean region. The fresh leaves are cooked like spinach in a variety of ways, and they are dried and used in smaller quantities to flavor meat and poultry dishes. Fenugreek seeds are used to flavor vegetables, lentils, and some fish dishes. They have a distinctive flavor and powerful taste, and should be used only in minute quantities.

Fish sauce

Fish sauce is one of the most commonly used ingredients in Southeast Asian cooking, especially Thailand, where it is known as *nam pla*. It is made from anchovies packed with liquid salt; the liquid that is eventually released by the fish is collected and sold as fish sauce. It enhances the overall flavors of Southeast Asian curries.

Galangal

This comes in two varieties: Greater galangal, also known as Laos ginger or Thai ginger, and lesser galangal. The former is more widely available and is an essential ingredient in most Southeast Asian curries, especially in Thailand. It has a creamy white flesh with a pine-like aroma. Lesser galangal, with its orange-tinged flesh, has a stronger and hotter flavor.

Garam masala

The word *garam* means "heat" and *masala* refers to the blending of different spices. They are believed to create body heat. The basic ingredients are cinnamon, cardamom, cloves, and black pepper. Other spices are added to these, according to preference.

Garlic

Fresh garlic is an integral part of Asian cooking. Dried flakes, powder, and garlic salt cannot create the same authentic flavor. It is always used crushed, finely chopped, or made into a paste. Garlic is beneficial in reducing the level of cholesterol in the blood and its antiseptic properties aid the digestive system.

To make garlic paste, peel a good quantity (at least 6 large bulbs) of garlic and process the cloves in a blender. To store in the refrigerator for immediate use, preserve the paste in cooking oil and store in an airtight jar. It will keep for 3–4 weeks. Alternatively, divide into small portions, freeze, and use as required. You can, of course, buy prepared garlic paste, but the homemade version has a superior flavor.

Ghee

Ghee has a rich and distinctive flavor and is used liberally in Mogul food. There are two types of ghee: Pure butterfat ghee and vegetable ghee. Butterfat ghee is made from unsalted butter and vegetable ghee from vegetable shortening. Ghee can be heated to a high temperature without burning. Both types of ghee are available from Indian stores and larger supermarkets. Unsalted butter can be used in some dishes, but cannot be heated to the same temperature.

Ginger

Like garlic, fresh ginger is essential in making curries. Ginger has a warm, woody aroma. On the medicinal side, ginger is believed to improve circulation of the blood and reduce acidity in the stomach. Dry ginger is used in some dishes, although not in curries.

To make ginger paste, peel the ginger using a potato peeler or scrape off the skin with a small sharp knife. Once peeled, chop coarsely and process in a blender. To store in the refrigerator for immediate use, preserve the paste in cooking oil and store in an airtight jar. It will keep for 3–4 weeks. Alternatively, divide into small portions, freeze, and use as required. If you buy prepared ginger paste, make sure it is preserved in oil and not citric acid, which tends to impair the flavor.

Jaggery

This dark, coarse, and unrefined sugar is made from the sap of the coconut palm tree. It is also referred to as palm sugar. It has a sweet wine-like flavor and usually comes in the form of a solid cake with a crumbly texture.

Lemongrass

Lemongrass has an intensely lemony flavor without the acidity of the fruit. It is widely used in Southeast Asian curries, soups, curry pastes, and pickles. Dried and ground lemongrass, known as "serai powder," makes a good alternative to fresh. Fresh lemongrass can be frozen successfully.

Limes/kaffir lime leaves

Kaffir limes are widely used throughout Southeast Asia. They lend an intense citrus bouquet to curries and curry pastes. The leaves can be used whole or finely shredded, and the latter method imparts a superior flavor. They can be frozen and used as required.

Mustard seeds

Mustard seeds are an essential ingredient in vegetarian cooking. Black and brown mustard seeds are the ones most commonly used, with the white ones being reserved for making pickles. Black and brown seeds lend a nutty flavor to the dish.

Nigella seeds

These tiny black seeds are also known as onion seeds because of their striking resemblance. The seeds are used whole for flavoring vegetables, pickles, breads, and snacks.

Peppercorns

Fresh green berries are dried in the sun to obtain black pepper. Green berries come from the pepper vine native to the monsoon forests of Southwest India. Whole black peppercorns will keep well in an airtight jar, but ground black pepper loses its wonderful aromatic flavor very quickly—it is best to store whole peppercorns in a pepper mill and grind as needed.

Poppy seeds

The opium poppy, grown mainly in the tropics, produces the best poppy seeds. There are two varieties: white and black. The white seeds are ground and added to curries to give them a nutty flavor. They are also used as a thickener and as a topping for naan.

Rose water

Rose water is the diluted extract of a special strain of edible rose, the petals of which are used to garnish Mogul dishes. Rose extract is more concentrated and only a few drops are needed if it is used instead of rose water.

Saffron

The saffron crocus grows extensively in Kashmir in northern India. Around 250,000 stamens of this crocus are needed to produce just 1 lb/450 g of saffron. It is a highly concentrated ingredient and only minute quantities are required to flavor and color any dish.

Shrimp paste

A popular ingredient in Southeast Asian curries, shrimp paste is made from fermented shrimp pounded with salt into a paste. It is also known as "terasi," "blachan," and "balachan" and it has a strong, fishy, and salty flavor.

Sesame seeds

These pale seeds have a rich and nutty flavor. They are native to India, which is the largest exporter of sesame oil to the West. They may be sprinkled on naan before baking, ground to a paste and used to thicken sauces, and used with vegetables and some sweet dishes.

Tamarind

Resembling pea pods at first, tamarind turns dark brown with a thin hard outer shell when ripe. The chocolate-brown flesh is encased in the shell with seeds, which have to be removed. The flesh is sold dried and has to be soaked in hot water to yield a pulp. Ready-to-use concentrated tamarind pulp or juice is quick and easy to use. Valued for its distinctive flavor, tamarind is added to vegetables, lentils, peas, chutneys, and many fish and shellfish dishes.

Turmeric

Fresh turmeric rhizomes resemble fresh ginger, with a beige-brown skin and bright yellow flesh. Fresh turmeric is dried and ground to produce this essential spice, which should be used in carefully measured quantities to prevent a bitter taste.

Essential recipes

1 tbsp coriander seeds
1 tbsp cumin seeds
12 fresh green Thai chiles, chopped
5 garlic cloves, chopped
2 lemongrass stalks, chopped
5 fresh kaffir lime leaves, chopped
handful of fresh cilantro, chopped
finely grated rind of 1 lime
1 tsp salt
1 tsp black peppercorns, crushed

THAI GREEN CURRY PASTE

Heat a dry skillet until hot, add the coriander and cumin seeds, and cook over medium–high heat, shaking the skillet frequently, for 2–3 minutes, or until they start to pop. Put the toasted seeds with all the remaining ingredients in a food processor or small blender and process to a thick, smooth paste. Transfer to a screw-top glass jar and store in the refrigerator for up to a week.

1 tbsp coriander seeds
1 tbsp cumin seeds
12 dried red chiles, chopped
2 shallots, chopped
6 garlic cloves, chopped
1-inch/2.5-cm piece fresh ginger, chopped
2 lemongrass stalks, chopped
4 fresh kaffir lime leaves, chopped
handful of fresh cilantro, chopped
finely grated rind of 1 lime
1 tsp salt
1 tsp black peppercorns, crushed

THAI RED CURRY PASTE

Heat a dry skillet until hot, add the coriander and cumin seeds, and cook over medium–high heat, shaking the skillet frequently, for 2–3 minutes, or until they start to pop. Put the toasted seeds with all the remaining ingredients in a food processor or small blender and process to a thick, smooth paste. Transfer to a screw-top glass jar and store in the refrigerator for up to a week.

3 small fresh orange or yellow chiles, chopped
3 garlic cloves, chopped
4 shallots, chopped
1 tbsp ground turmeric
1 tsp salt
12–15 black peppercorns, crushed
1 lemongrass stalk (white part only), chopped
1-inch/2.5-cm piece fresh ginger, chopped

THAI YELLOW CURRY PASTE

Put all the ingredients in a food processor or small blender and process to a thick, smooth paste. Transfer to a screw-top glass jar and store in the refrigerator for up to a week.

MUSSAMAN CURRY PASTE

4 large dried red chiles
2 tsp shrimp paste
3 shallots, finely chopped
3 garlic cloves, finely chopped
1-inch/2.5-cm piece fresh galangal, chopped
2 lemongrass stalks (white part only), finely chopped
2 cloves
1 tbsp coriander seeds
1 tbsp cumin seeds
seeds from 3 green cardamom pods
1 tsp black peppercorns
1 tsp salt

Cut off and discard the chile stalks and place the chiles in a bowl. Cover with hot water and soak for 30–45 minutes. Wrap the shrimp paste in foil and broil or dry-fry for 2–3 minutes, turning once or twice. Remove from the broiler or skillet. Dry-fry the shallots, garlic, galangal, lemongrass, cloves, coriander seeds, cumin seeds, and cardamom seeds over low heat, stirring frequently, for 3–4 minutes, until lightly browned. Transfer to a food processor and process until finely ground. Add the chiles and their soaking water and the peppercorns and salt, and process again. Add the shrimp paste and process again to a smooth paste. Transfer to a screw-top glass jar and store in the refrigerator for up to a week.

PENANG CURRY PASTE

8 large dried red chiles
2 tsp shrimp paste
3 shallots, chopped
2-inch/5-cm piece fresh galangal, chopped
8 garlic cloves, chopped
4 tbsp chopped cilantro root
3 lemongrass stalks (white part only), chopped
grated rind of 1 lime
1 tbsp fish sauce
2 tbsp vegetable oil or peanut oil
1 tsp salt
6 tbsp crunchy peanut butter

Cut off and discard the chile stalks and place the chiles in a bowl. Cover with hot water and soak for 30–45 minutes. Wrap the shrimp paste in foil and broil or dry-fry for 2–3 minutes, turning once or twice. Put the chiles and their soaking water into a blender or food processor. Add the shrimp paste, shallots, galangal, garlic, cilantro root, and lemongrass and process until finely chopped. Add the lime rind, Thai fish sauce, oil, and salt and process again. Add the peanut butter and process to make a thick paste. Transfer to a screw-top glass jar and store in the refrigerator for up to a week.

GARLIC AND GINGER PASTE

1–2 garlic bulbs, separated into cloves, coarsely chopped
large piece fresh ginger, coarsely chopped

Put equal quantities of garlic and ginger in a food processor or small blender and process to a smooth paste. Transfer to a screw-top glass jar and store in the refrigerator for up to a week.

GARAM MASALA

2 bay leaves, crumbled
2 cinnamon sticks, broken in half
seeds from 8 green cardamom
pods
2 tbsp cumin seeds
1½ tbsp coriander seeds
1½ tsp black peppercorns
1 tsp cloves
¼ tsp ground cloves

Heat a dry skillet over high heat until a splash of water "dances" when it hits the surface. Reduce the heat to medium, add the bay leaves, cinnamon sticks, cardamom seeds, cumin seeds, coriander seeds, peppercorns, and whole cloves, and dry-fry, stirring continuously, until the cumin seeds look dark golden brown and you can smell the aromas. Immediately turn the spices out of the skillet and let cool. Use a spice grinder or pestle and mortar to grind the spices to a fine powder. Stir in the ground cloves. Store in an airtight container for up to two months.

GHEE

generous 1 cup butter

Melt the butter in a large heavy saucepan over medium heat and continue simmering until a thick foam appears on the surface. Continue simmering, uncovered, for 15–20 minutes, or until the foam separates and the milk solids settle on the bottom and the liquid becomes clear and golden.

Meanwhile, line a strainer with a piece of cheesecloth and place the strainer over a bowl. Slowly pour the liquid through the cheesecloth, without disturbing the milk solids at the bottom of the pan. Discard the milk solids.

Let the ghee cool, then transfer to a smaller container, cover, and chill. Store in the refrigerator for up to four weeks.

PANEER

10 cups milk
6 tbsp lemon juice

Pour the milk into a large heavy saucepan and bring to a boil over high heat. Remove the pan from the heat and stir in the lemon juice. Return to the heat and continue boiling for an additional minute, until the curds and whey separate and the liquid is clear.

Remove the pan from the heat and set aside for about 1 hour, until the milk is completely cool. Meanwhile, line a strainer with a piece of cheesecloth large enough to hang over the edge and place the strainer over a bowl.

Pour the curds and whey into the cheesecloth, then gather up the edges and squeeze out all the excess moisture.

Use a piece of string to tie the cheesecloth tightly around the curds in a ball. Put the ball in a bowl and place a plate on top. Place a food can on the plate to weigh down the curds, then chill in the refrigerator for at least 12 hours. The curds will press into a compact mass that can be cut. The paneer will keep for up to three days in the refrigerator.

Chicken

Chicken Tikka Masala

This Indian dish reputedly started life in London restaurants as a way to use up leftover cooked tandoori chicken. It has now gone full cycle and is prepared in Indian restaurants. The quickest way to make this is to buy cooked tandoori chicken pieces from a supermarket or an Indian takeout. If, however, you want to make your own tandoori chicken, follow the recipe on page 22, then cut the cooked bird into pieces.

SERVES 4-6

14 oz/400 g canned chopped tomatoes

1¼ cups heavy cream

1 cooked tandoori chicken,
    cut into 8 pieces

salt and pepper

fresh chopped cilantro, to garnish

cooked basmati rice, to serve

TIKKA MASALA

2 tbsp ghee, vegetable oil, or peanut oil

1 large garlic clove, finely chopped

1 fresh red chile, seeded and chopped

2 tsp ground cumin

2 tsp ground paprika

½ tsp salt

pepper

To make the tikka masala, melt the ghee in a large skillet with a lid over medium heat. Add the garlic and chile and stir-fry for 1 minute. Stir in the cumin, paprika, and salt and pepper to taste and continue stirring for about 30 seconds.

Stir the tomatoes and cream into the skillet. Reduce the heat to low and let the sauce simmer for about 10 minutes, stirring frequently, until it reduces and thickens.

Meanwhile, remove all the bones and any skin from the tandoori chicken pieces, then cut the meat into bite-size pieces.

Adjust the seasoning of the sauce, if necessary. Add the chicken pieces to the skillet, cover, and let simmer for 3–5 minutes, until the chicken is heated through. Garnish with cilantro and serve with cooked basmati rice.

Tandoori Chicken

Don't expect to duplicate this dish exactly as it is served at your favorite Indian restaurant. That's impossible to do at home—unless you happen to have a tandoor oven in the kitchen—but this comes close, especially if you let the bird marinate for a day before cooking. Indian cooks add the bright red-orange color to tandoori dishes with natural food colorings, such as cochineal. A few drops of synthetic food coloring are a more readily available option for most home cooks. Kashmiri chili powder will also enhance the red color.

SERVES 4

1 chicken, weighing 3 lb 5 oz/1.5 kg, skinned

½ lemon

1 tsp salt

2 tbsp ghee, melted

fresh cilantro sprigs, to garnish

lemon wedges, to serve

TANDOORI MASALA PASTE

1 tbsp garlic and ginger paste

1 tbsp ground paprika

1 tsp ground cinnamon

1 tsp ground cumin

½ tsp ground coriander

¼ tsp chili powder, ideally Kashmiri chili powder

pinch of ground cloves

¼ tsp edible red food coloring (optional)

few drops of edible yellow food coloring (optional)

generous ¾ cup plain yogurt

To make the tandoori masala paste, combine the garlic and ginger paste, dry spices, and food coloring, if using, in a bowl and stir in the yogurt. You can use the paste now or store it in an airtight container in the refrigerator for up to three days.

Use a small knife to make thin cuts all over the chicken. Rub the lemon half over the chicken, then rub the salt into the cuts. Put the chicken in a deep bowl, add the paste, and use your hands to rub it all over the bird and into the cuts. Cover the bowl with plastic wrap and refrigerate for at least 4 hours, but ideally up to 24 hours.

When you are ready to cook the chicken, preheat the oven to 400°F/200°C. Put the chicken on a rack in a roasting pan, breast-side up, and drizzle over the melted ghee. Roast in the preheated oven for 45 minutes, then quickly remove the bird and roasting pan from the oven and increase the oven temperature to high.

Very carefully pour out any fat from the bottom of the roasting pan. Return the chicken to the oven and roast for an additional 10–15 minutes, until the juices run clear when you pierce the thigh with a knife and the paste is lightly charred.

Let stand for 10 minutes, then cut into pieces. Garnish with cilantro sprigs and serve with lemon wedges.

COOK'S TIP

For a quicker version, use chicken breasts, thighs, or drumsticks. Marinate as above, preheat the oven to 450°F/230°C, and roast for about 40 minutes.

Pistachio Chicken Korma

It is a common misconception that korma is a mild and creamy dish. In fact, korma is not a dish but one of the several techniques used in Indian cooking. This delectable korma from Delhi has an unusual and irresistible aroma and taste.

SERVES 4

¾ cup shelled pistachios

scant 1 cup boiling water

good pinch of saffron threads, pounded

2 tbsp hot milk

1 lb 9 oz/700 g skinless, boneless
   chicken breasts or thighs, cut into
   1-inch/2.5-cm cubes

1 tsp salt, or to taste

½ tsp pepper

juice of ½ lemon

4 tbsp ghee or unsalted butter

6 green cardamom pods

1 large onion, finely chopped

2 tsp garlic paste

2 tsp ginger paste

1 tbsp ground coriander

½ tsp chili powder

1¼ cups plain yogurt, whisked

⅔ cup light cream

2 tbsp rose water

6–8 white rose petals, washed,
   to garnish

cooked basmati rice and lemon wedges,
   to serve

Soak the pistachios in the boiling water in a heatproof bowl for 20 minutes. Meanwhile, soak the saffron in the hot milk.

Put the chicken in a nonmetallic bowl and add the salt, pepper, and lemon juice. Rub into the chicken, cover, and let marinate in the refrigerator for 30 minutes.

Melt the ghee in a medium heavy-bottom saucepan over low heat and add the cardamom pods. When they have puffed up, add the onion and increase the heat to medium. Cook, stirring frequently, for 8–9 minutes, until the onion is a pale golden color.

Add the garlic paste and ginger paste and cook, stirring frequently, for an additional 2–3 minutes. Add the coriander and chili powder and cook, stirring, for 30 seconds. Add the chicken, increase the heat to medium–high, and cook, stirring continuously, for 5–6 minutes, until it changes color.

Reduce the heat to low and add the yogurt and the saffron and milk mixture. Bring to a slow simmer, cover, and cook for 15 minutes. Stir halfway through to ensure that it does not stick to the bottom of the pan.

Meanwhile, put the pistachios and their soaking water in a blender or food processor and process until smooth. Add to the chicken mixture, followed by the cream. Cover and simmer, stirring occasionally, for an additional 15–20 minutes. Stir in the rose water and remove from the heat. Garnish with the rose petals and serve immediately with cooked basmati rice and lemon wedges.

Kashmiri Chicken

This mild and aromatic Kashmiri dish is delicately flavored and colored with saffron threads, grown in the northern region. Chicken thighs are used in this recipe, but any pieces of boneless meat are suitable.

SERVES 4-6

seeds from 8 green cardamom pods

½ tsp coriander seeds

½ tsp cumin seeds

1 cinnamon stick

8 black peppercorns

6 cloves

1 tbsp hot water

½ tsp saffron threads

3 tbsp ghee, vegetable oil, or peanut oil

1 large onion, finely chopped

2 tbsp garlic and ginger paste

generous 1 cup plain yogurt

8 skinless, boneless chicken thighs, sliced

3 tbsp ground almonds

generous ⅓ cup blanched pistachios, finely chopped

2 tbsp chopped fresh cilantro

2 tbsp chopped fresh mint

salt

toasted slivered almonds, to garnish

Indian bread, to serve

Dry-roast the cardamom seeds in a hot skillet over medium–low heat, stirring continuously, until you can smell the aroma. Immediately tip them out of the skillet so they don't burn. Repeat with the coriander and cumin seeds, cinnamon stick, peppercorns, and cloves. Put all the spices, except the cinnamon stick, in a spice grinder, or use a pestle and mortar, and grind to a powder.

Put the hot water and saffron threads in a small bowl and set aside.

Melt the ghee in a flameproof casserole or large skillet with a tight-fitting lid over medium–high heat. Add the onion and sauté, stirring occasionally, for 5–8 minutes, until it becomes golden brown. Add the garlic and ginger paste and continue stirring for 2 minutes.

Stir in the ground spices and the cinnamon stick. Remove from the heat and mix in the yogurt, a small amount at a time, stirring vigorously with each addition, then return to the heat and continue stirring for 2–3 minutes, until the ghee separates. Add the chicken pieces.

Bring the mixture to a boil, stirring continuously, then reduce the heat to the lowest setting, cover the casserole, and simmer for 20 minutes, stirring occasionally and checking that the mixture isn't catching on the bottom of the casserole. If it does start to catch, stir in a little water.

Stir the ground almonds, pistachios, saffron liquid, half the cilantro, all the mint, and salt to taste into the chicken mixture. Re-cover the casserole and continue simmering for about 5 minutes, until the chicken is tender and the sauce is thickened. Sprinkle with the remaining cilantro, garnish with slivered almonds, and serve with Indian bread.

Butter Chicken

As with Chicken Tikka Masala, the quickest way to prepare this popular Sikh dish is to buy prepared tandoori chicken. Otherwise, start with the Tandoori Chicken recipe on page 22. This is a good party dish, with a rich, creamy sauce that you can make as hot as you like, depending on the amount of chili powder you include.

SERVES 4-6

1 onion, chopped

1½ tbsp garlic and ginger paste

14 oz/400 g canned chopped tomatoes

¼–½ tsp chili powder

pinch of sugar

2 tbsp ghee, vegetable oil, or peanut oil

½ cup water

1 tbsp tomato paste

3 tbsp butter, cut into small pieces

½ tsp garam masala

½ tsp ground cumin

½ tsp ground coriander

1 cooked tandoori chicken,
    cut into 8 pieces

4 tbsp heavy cream

salt and pepper

chopped cashew nuts and fresh cilantro
    sprigs, to garnish

Put the onion and the garlic and ginger paste in a food processor, blender, or spice grinder and process until a paste forms. Add the tomatoes, chili powder, sugar, and a pinch of salt and process again until blended.

Melt the ghee in a wok or large skillet over medium–high heat. Add the tomato mixture and water, stirring in the tomato paste.

Bring the mixture to a boil, stirring, then reduce the heat to very low and simmer for 5 minutes, stirring occasionally, until the sauce thickens.

Stir in half the butter, the garam masala, cumin, and coriander. Add the chicken pieces and stir until they are well coated. Simmer for about an additional 10 minutes, or until the chicken is hot. Taste and adjust the seasoning, if necessary.

Lightly beat the cream in a small bowl and stir in several tablespoons of the hot sauce, beating continuously. Stir the cream mixture into the tomato sauce, then add the remaining butter and stir until it melts. Garnish with the chopped cashew nuts and cilantro sprigs and serve straight from the wok.

Chicken Biryani

In this dish from the snow-fed foothills of the Himalayas, the naturally fragrant basmati rice is enhanced with cinnamon, cardamom, and star anise, and layered with delicately spiced chicken. It is cooked in a sealed pot to conserve the flavors.

SERVES 4–5

⅓ cup whole milk plain yogurt

1 tbsp garlic paste

1 tbsp ginger paste

1 lb 9 oz/700 g skinless, boneless
   chicken thighs

1 tbsp white poppy seeds

2 tsp coriander seeds

½ mace blade

2 bay leaves, torn into small pieces

½ tsp black peppercorns

1 tsp green cardamom seeds

1-inch/2.5-cm piece cinnamon stick,
   broken up

4 cloves

4 tbsp ghee or unsalted butter

1 large onion, finely sliced

1½ tsp salt, or to taste

RICE

pinch of saffron threads, pounded

2 tbsp hot milk

1½ tsp salt

2 x 2-inch/5-cm cinnamon sticks

3 star anise

2 bay leaves, crumbled

4 cloves

4 green cardamom pods, bruised

1 lb/450 g basmati rice, washed

TO GARNISH

2 tbsp sunflower oil

1 onion, finely sliced

Put the yogurt, garlic paste, and ginger paste into a bowl and beat together with a fork until thoroughly blended. Put the chicken in a nonmetallic bowl, add the yogurt mixture, and mix until well blended. Cover and let marinate in the refrigerator for 2 hours.

Grind the next eight ingredients (all the seeds and spices) to a fine powder in a coffee grinder and set aside. In an ovenproof casserole large enough to hold the chicken and the rice together, melt the ghee over medium heat, add the onion, and cook, stirring frequently, for 8–10 minutes, until a medium brown color. Reduce the heat to low, add the ground ingredients, and cook, stirring, for 2–3 minutes. Add the marinated chicken and salt and cook, stirring, for 2 minutes. Turn off the heat and keep the chicken covered.

To make the rice, soak the saffron in the hot milk for 20 minutes. Preheat the oven to 350°F/180°C. Bring a large saucepan of water to a boil and add the salt and spices. Add the rice, return to a boil, and boil steadily for 2 minutes. Drain the rice, reserving the whole spices, and pile on top of the chicken. Pour the saffron and milk over the rice.

Soak a piece of wax paper large enough to cover the top of the rice fully and squeeze out the excess water. Lay on top of the rice. Soak a clean dish towel, wring out, and lay loosely on top of the wax paper. Cover the casserole with a piece of foil. It is important to cover the rice in this way to contain all the steam inside the casserole, as the biryani cooks entirely in the vapor created inside the casserole. Put the lid on top and cook in the center of the preheated oven for 1 hour. Turn off the oven and let the rice stand inside for 30 minutes.

Meanwhile, heat the oil for the garnish in a small saucepan over medium heat, add the onion, and cook, stirring, for 12–15 minutes, until browned. Transfer the biryani to a serving dish and garnish with the fried onions.

Chicken Dopiaza

The meaning of dopiaza *remains controversial. It is widely believed to mean a dish with twice the normal amount of onions, but connoisseurs of Mogul food argue that it is a Mogul term meaning any meat or poultry cooked with vegetables.*

SERVES 4

1 lb 9 oz/700 g skinless, boneless
   chicken breasts or thighs

juice of ½ lemon

1 tsp salt, or to taste

5 tbsp sunflower oil or olive oil

2 large onions, coarsely chopped

5 large garlic cloves, coarsely chopped

1-inch/2.5-cm piece fresh ginger,
   coarsely chopped

2 tbsp plain yogurt

1-inch/2.5-cm piece cinnamon stick,
   halved

4 green cardamom pods, bruised

4 cloves

½ tsp black peppercorns

½ tsp ground turmeric

½–1 tsp chili powder

1 tsp ground coriander

4 tbsp canned crushed tomatoes

⅔ cup warm water

½ tsp sugar

8 shallots, halved

1 tsp garam masala

2 tbsp chopped fresh cilantro leaves

1 tomato, chopped

Indian bread, to serve

Cut the chicken into 1-inch/2.5-cm cubes and put in a nonmetallic bowl. Add the lemon juice and half the salt and rub well into the chicken. Cover and let marinate in the refrigerator for 20 minutes.

Heat 1 tablespoon of the oil in a small saucepan over medium heat, add the onions, garlic, and ginger, and cook, stirring frequently, for 4–5 minutes. Remove from the heat and let cool slightly. Transfer the ingredients to a blender or food processor, add the yogurt, and blend to a paste.

Heat 3 tablespoons of the remaining oil in a medium heavy-bottom saucepan over low heat, add the cinnamon stick, cardamom pods, cloves, and peppercorns, and cook, stirring, for 25–30 seconds. Add the processed ingredients, increase the heat to medium, and cook, stirring frequently, for 5 minutes.

Add the turmeric, chili powder, and coriander and cook, stirring, for 2 minutes. Add the tomatoes and cook, stirring, for 3 minutes. Increase the heat slightly, then add the marinated chicken and cook, stirring, until it changes color. Add the warm water, the remaining salt, and the sugar. Bring to a boil, then reduce the heat to low, cover, and cook for 10 minutes. Remove the lid and cook, uncovered, for an additional 10 minutes, or until the sauce thickens.

Meanwhile, heat the remaining oil in a small saucepan, add the shallots, and stir-fry until browned and separated. Add the garam masala and cook, stirring, for 30 seconds. Stir the shallot mixture into the curry and simmer for 2 minutes. Stir in the fresh cilantro and chopped tomato and remove from the heat. Serve immediately with Indian bread.

Chicken Jalfrezi

The popular jalfrezi was created during the British Raj to use up cold cooked meat. This recipe comes from Kolkata (previously Calcutta), where jalfrezi was frequently served to the members of the East India Company.

SERVES 4

1 lb 9 oz/700 g skinless, boneless chicken breasts or thighs

juice of ½ lemon

1 tsp salt, or to taste

5 tbsp sunflower oil or olive oil

1 large onion, finely chopped

2 tsp garlic paste

2 tsp ginger paste

½ tsp ground turmeric

1 tsp ground cumin

2 tsp ground coriander

½–1 tsp chili powder

5½ oz/150 g canned chopped tomatoes

⅔ cup warm water

1 large garlic clove, finely chopped

1 small or ½ large red bell pepper, seeded and cut into 1-inch/2.5-cm pieces

1 small or ½ large green bell pepper, seeded and cut into 1-inch/2.5-cm pieces

1 tsp garam masala

Indian bread or cooked basmati rice, to serve

Cut the chicken into 1-inch/2.5-cm cubes and put in a nonmetallic bowl. Add the lemon juice and half the salt and rub well into the chicken. Cover and let marinate in the refrigerator for 20 minutes.

Heat 4 tablespoons of the oil in a medium heavy-bottom saucepan over medium heat. Add the onion and cook, stirring frequently, for 8–9 minutes, until lightly browned. Add the garlic paste and ginger paste and cook, stirring, for 3 minutes. Add the turmeric, cumin, coriander, and chili powder and cook, stirring, for 1 minute. Add the tomatoes and cook for 2–3 minutes, stirring frequently, until the oil separates from the spice paste.

Add the marinated chicken, increase the heat slightly, and cook, stirring, until it changes color. Add the warm water and bring to a boil. Reduce the heat, cover, and simmer for 25 minutes.

Heat the remaining oil in a small saucepan or skillet over low heat. Add the garlic and cook, stirring frequently, until browned. Add the bell peppers, increase the heat to medium, and stir-fry for 2 minutes, then stir in the garam masala. Fold the bell pepper mixture into the curry. Remove from the heat and serve immediately with Indian bread or cooked basmati rice.

Creamy Chicken Tikka

There are several versions of this ever-popular dish, and this one is quite special. Grated mild cheddar cheese and cream are added to the marinade, and the combination of the dairy ingredients has a magical effect in tenderizing the meat.

SERVES 4

1 lb 9 oz/700 g skinless, boneless
   chicken breasts, cut into 1-inch/2.5-cm
   cubes

2 tbsp lemon juice

½ tsp salt, or to taste

½ cup whole milk strained plain yogurt,
   or Greek-style yogurt

3 tbsp heavy cream

1 oz/25 g mild cheddar cheese, grated

1 tbsp garlic paste

1 tbsp ginger paste

½–1 tsp chili powder

½ tsp ground turmeric

½ tsp sugar

1 tbsp chickpea flour, sifted

1 tsp garam masala

2 tbsp sunflower oil or olive oil,
   plus 2 tbsp for brushing

3 tbsp melted butter or olive oil

salad and chutney, to serve

Put the chicken in a nonmetallic bowl and add the lemon juice and salt. Rub well into the chicken. Cover and let marinate in the refrigerator for 20–30 minutes.

Put the yogurt in a separate nonmetallic bowl and beat with a fork until smooth. Add all the remaining ingredients, except the melted butter. Beat well until the ingredients are fully incorporated. Add the chicken and mix thoroughly until fully coated with the marinade. Cover and let marinate in the refrigerator for 4–6 hours, or overnight. Return to room temperature before cooking.

Preheat the broiler to high. Brush 6 metal skewers generously with the remaining 2 tablespoons of oil and thread on the chicken cubes. Brush over any remaining marinade. Place the prepared skewers in a broiler pan and broil about 3 inches/7.5 cm below the heat source for 4–5 minutes. Brush generously with the melted butter and cook for an additional 1–2 minutes. Turn over and cook for 3–4 minutes, basting frequently with the remaining melted butter.

Balance the skewers over a large saucepan or frying pan and leave to rest for 5–6 minutes before sliding the chicken cubes off the skewers with a knife. Serve with salad and chutney.

Vietnamese Chicken Curry

This Vietnamese chicken curry is delicate in comparison to the more widely known Thai curries. The sweet and savory broth is coconut milk seasoned with Indian curry powder, fish sauce, and lemongrass.

SERVES 6

2 lemongrass stalks

¼ cup vegetable oil

3 large garlic cloves, crushed

1 large shallot, thinly sliced

2 tbsp Indian curry powder

3 cups coconut milk

2 cups coconut water (not coconut milk)
   or chicken stock

2 tbsp fish sauce

4 fresh red Thai chiles or dried red
   Chinese (tien sien) chiles

6 kaffir lime leaves

6 boneless chicken thighs or breasts,
   6–8 oz/175–225 g each, with or
   without skin, cut into 2-inch/5-cm
   pieces

1 large white yam or sweet potato,
   peeled and cut into 1-inch/2.5-cm
   chunks

2 Asian eggplants, cut into
   1-inch/2.5-cm pieces

2 cups green beans, trimmed

2 carrots, peeled and diagonally cut into
   ½ inch/1 cm thick pieces

fresh Thai basil sprigs, to garnish

cooked jasmine rice, to serve

Discard the bruised leaves and root ends of the lemongrass stalks, then cut 6–8 inches/15–20 cm of the lower stalks into paper-thin slices.

Heat the oil in a large saucepan over high heat, then add the garlic and shallot, and stir-fry for 5 minutes, or until golden. Add the lemongrass and curry powder and stir-fry for 2 minutes, or until fragrant. Add the coconut milk, coconut water, fish sauce, chiles, and lime leaves and bring to a boil. Reduce the heat to low and add the chicken, yam, eggplants, green beans, and carrots. Simmer, covered, for 1 hour, or until the chicken and vegetables are tender and the flavors have blended.

Serve garnished with Thai basil sprigs and accompanied by cooked jasmine rice.

Thai Green Chicken Curry

The fiery taste of this fragrant Thai-style curry is mellowed by cooling coconut milk and delicately aromatic herbs. While there are many excellent commercial curry pastes available, it's still worth the effort of making your own (see page 14 for the recipe)—the results will speak for themselves.

SERVES 4

2 tbsp peanut oil or corn oil

2 tbsp Thai green curry paste

1 lb 2 oz/500 g skinless, boneless chicken breasts, cut into cubes

2 kaffir lime leaves, coarsely torn

1 lemongrass stalk, finely chopped

1 cup coconut milk

16 baby eggplants, halved

2 tbsp fish sauce

fresh Thai basil sprigs and thinly sliced kaffir lime leaves, to garnish

Heat the oil in a preheated wok or large heavy-bottom skillet. Add the curry paste and stir-fry briefly until all the aromas are released.

Add the chicken, lime leaves, and lemongrass and stir-fry for 3–4 minutes, until the meat is beginning to color. Add the coconut milk and eggplants and simmer gently for 8–10 minutes, or until tender.

Stir in the fish sauce and serve immediately garnished with Thai basil sprigs and lime leaves.

Penang Chicken Curry

This delicious curry dish uses Penang curry paste (see page 15 for the recipe), a Malaysian-influenced paste that is very similar to Thai red curry paste except that it contains peanuts.

SERVES 4

1 tbsp vegetable oil or peanut oil

2 red onions, sliced

2 tbsp Penang curry paste

1¾ cups coconut milk

⅔ cup chicken stock

4 kaffir lime leaves, coarsely torn

1 lemongrass stalk, finely chopped

6 skinless, boneless chicken thighs, chopped

1 tbsp fish sauce

2 tbsp Thai soy sauce

1 tsp jaggery or light brown sugar

½ cup unsalted peanuts, roasted and chopped, plus extra to garnish

6 oz/175 g fresh pineapple, coarsely chopped

6-inch/15-cm piece cucumber, peeled, seeded, and thickly sliced, plus extra to garnish

Heat the oil in a wok and stir-fry the onions for 1 minute. Add the curry paste and stir-fry for 1–2 minutes.

Pour in the coconut milk and stock. Add the lime leaves and lemongrass and let simmer for 1 minute. Add the chicken and gradually bring to a boil. Let simmer for 8–10 minutes, until the chicken is tender.

Stir in the fish sauce, soy sauce, and jaggery, and let simmer for 1–2 minutes. Stir in the peanuts, pineapple, and cucumber, and cook for 30 seconds. Serve immediately, sprinkled with extra peanuts and cucumber.

Shredded Chicken & Mixed Mushrooms

Chicken and mushrooms are a magical combination and look fantastic studded with emerald green flecks of parsley. For maximum flavor, make sure to use a mixture of different mushrooms.

SERVES 4

2 tbsp vegetable oil or peanut oil

2 skinless, boneless chicken breasts

1 red onion, sliced

2 garlic cloves, finely chopped

1-inch/2.5-cm piece fresh ginger, grated

4 oz/115 g button mushrooms

4 oz/115 g shiitake mushrooms, halved

4 oz/115 g cremini mushrooms, sliced

2–3 tbsp Thai green curry paste

2 tbsp Thai soy sauce

4 tbsp chopped fresh parsley

cooked noodles or rice, to serve

Heat the oil in a wok and cook the chicken on all sides until lightly browned and cooked through. Remove with a slotted spoon, shred into equal-size pieces, and set aside.

Pour off any excess oil, then stir-fry the onion, garlic, and ginger for 1–2 minutes, until softened. Add the mushrooms and stir-fry for 2–3 minutes, until they start to brown.

Add the curry paste, soy sauce, and shredded chicken to the wok and stir-fry for 1–2 minutes. Stir in the parsley and serve immediately with cooked noodles or rice.

Thai Yellow Chicken Curry

Thai yellow curry paste is the mildest of the Thai curry pastes. This is a healthy version of the traditional Thai curry because it uses plain yogurt rather than coconut milk, which is high in fat.

SERVES 4
SPICE PASTE

6 tbsp Thai yellow curry paste

⅔ cup plain yogurt

1¾ cups water

handful of fresh cilantro, chopped, plus
    extra to garnish

handful of fresh Thai basil leaves,
    shredded, plus extra to garnish

STIR-FRY

2 tbsp vegetable oil or peanut oil

2 onions, cut into thin wedges

2 garlic cloves, finely chopped

2 skinless, boneless chicken breasts,
    cut into strips

6 oz/175 g baby corn, halved lengthwise

To make the spice paste, stir-fry the curry paste in a wok for 2–3 minutes, then stir in the yogurt, water, and herbs. Bring to a boil, then let simmer for 2–3 minutes.

Meanwhile, heat the oil in a wok and stir-fry the onions and garlic for 2–3 minutes. Add the chicken and corn and stir-fry for 3–4 minutes, until the meat and corn are tender.

Stir in the spice paste and bring to a boil. Let simmer for 2–3 minutes, until heated through. Serve immediately, garnished with extra herbs.

Chicken Curry with Fried Noodles

The rice noodles puff up really quickly in hot oil—great entertainment for children to watch at a safe distance—but take care, as they are done in a matter of seconds.

SERVES 4

2 tbsp peanut oil or vegetable oil, plus extra for deep-frying

4 skinless, boneless chicken breasts, about 4 oz/115 g each, cut into 1-inch/2.5-cm cubes

2 red onions, coarsely chopped

5 scallions, coarsely chopped

2 garlic cloves, finely chopped

1 fresh green chile, seeded and finely chopped

6 oz/175 g shiitake mushrooms, thickly sliced

2 tbsp Thai green curry paste

1¾ cups coconut milk

1¼ cups chicken stock

2 fresh kaffir lime leaves

handful of fresh cilantro, chopped

handful of fresh chives, snipped

1 oz/25 g stir-fry rice noodles

Heat the oil in a preheated wok. Add the chicken, in batches, and stir-fry over medium–high heat for 3–4 minutes, or until lightly browned all over. Remove with a slotted spoon, then transfer to a plate and set aside.

Add the red onions, scallions, garlic, and chile to the wok and stir-fry over medium heat, adding a little more oil if necessary, for 2–3 minutes, or until softened but not browned. Add the mushrooms and stir-fry over high heat for 30 seconds. Return the chicken to the wok.

Add the curry paste, coconut milk, stock, and lime leaves and bring gently to a boil, stirring occasionally. Reduce the heat and simmer gently for 4–5 minutes, or until the chicken is tender and cooked through. Stir in the cilantro and chives.

Meanwhile, heat the oil for deep-frying in a separate wok or deep-sided skillet to 350–375°F/180–190°C, or until a cube of bread browns in 30 seconds. Divide the noodles into four portions and cook, one portion at a time, for about 2 seconds, until puffed up and crisp. Remove with a slotted spoon and drain on paper towels.

Serve the curry topped with the crispy noodles.

Wok-Cooked Chicken in Tomato & Fenugreek Sauce

A delectable dish from northern India, which is cooked in the Indian-style wok (kadhai) and is known as kadhai murgh *in India. The tomato-and-onion-based sauce has the predominant flavor of dried fenugreek leaves (kasuri methi), the characteristic ingredient in the cuisine of this region. Chicken thighs have been used here as they have a more succulent taste, but breast portions can be used, if preferred.*

SERVES 4

1 lb 9 oz/700 g skinless, boneless chicken thighs, cut into 1-inch/2.5-cm cubes

juice of 1 lime

1 tsp salt, or to taste

4 tbsp sunflower oil or olive oil

1 large onion, finely chopped

2 tsp ginger paste

2 tsp garlic paste

½ tsp ground turmeric

½–1 tsp chili powder

1 tbsp ground coriander

15 oz/425 g canned chopped tomatoes

½ cup warm water

1 tbsp dried fenugreek leaves

½ tsp garam masala

2 tbsp chopped fresh cilantro leaves

2–4 fresh green chiles

Indian bread, to serve

Place the chicken in a nonmetallic bowl and rub in the lime juice and salt. Cover and set aside for 30 minutes.

Heat the oil in a wok or heavy skillet over medium–high heat. Add the onion and stir-fry for 7–8 minutes, until it begins to color.

Add the ginger and garlic pastes and continue to stir-fry for about a minute. Add the turmeric, chili powder, and ground coriander, then reduce the heat slightly, and cook the spices for 25–30 seconds. Add half the tomatoes, stir-fry for 3–4 minutes, and add the remaining tomatoes. Continue to cook, stirring, until the tomato juice has evaporated and the oil separates from the spice paste and floats on the surface.

Add the chicken and increase the heat to high. Stir-fry for 4–5 minutes, then add the warm water, reduce the heat to medium–low, and cook for 8–10 minutes, or until the sauce has thickened and the chicken is tender.

Add the fenugreek leaves, garam masala, half the cilantro leaves, and the chiles. Cook for 1–2 minutes, remove from the heat, and transfer to a serving plate. Garnish with the remaining cilantro and serve with Indian bread.

Cumin-Scented Chicken

Cumin-scented chicken or zeera murgh *is quick and easy to make and is wonderfully aromatic with cinnamon, cardamom, and cloves. The warm and assertive character of cumin plays the central role here, but is in complete harmony with all the other ingredients used.*

SERVES 4

1 lb 9 oz/700 g boneless chicken thighs
    or breasts, cut into 5-cm/2-inch pieces

juice of 1 lime

1 tsp salt, or to taste

3 tbsp sunflower oil or olive oil

1 tsp cumin seeds

1-inch/2.5-cm piece cinnamon stick

5 green cardamom pods, bruised

4 cloves

1 large onion, finely chopped

2 tsp garlic paste

2 tsp ginger paste

½ tsp ground turmeric

2 tsp ground cumin

½ tsp chili powder

8 oz/225 g canned chopped tomatoes

1 tbsp tomato paste

½ tsp sugar

1 cup warm water

½ tsp garam masala

2 tbsp chopped fresh cilantro leaves,
    plus extra sprigs to garnish

Indian bread, to serve

Put the chicken in a nonmetallic bowl and rub in the lime juice and salt. Cover and set aside for 30 minutes.

Heat the oil in a medium saucepan over low heat and add the cumin seeds, cinnamon, cardamom, and cloves. Let them sizzle for 25–30 seconds, then add the onion. Cook, stirring frequently, for 5 minutes, or until the onion has softened.

Add the garlic paste and ginger paste and cook for about a minute, then add the turmeric, ground cumin, and chili powder. Add the tomatoes, tomato paste, and sugar. Cook over medium heat, stirring frequently, until the tomatoes reach a paste-like consistency and the oil separates from the spice paste. Sprinkle over a little water if the mixture sticks to the pan.

Add the chicken and increase the heat to medium–high. Stir until the chicken changes color, then pour in the warm water. Bring to a boil, reduce the heat to medium–low, and cook for 12–15 minutes, or until the sauce has thickened and the chicken is tender.

Stir in the garam masala and chopped cilantro. Transfer to a serving dish and garnish with cilantro sprigs. Serve with Indian bread.

Chicken in Green Chile, Mint & Cilantro Sauce

When you cook this dish, it will remind you of a summer's garden and its appearance will delight you. The emerald green mixture of fresh green chiles, mint, and cilantro embraces the pieces of chicken, which are golden from the turmeric and aromatized with cardamom, cinnamon, and nutmeg.

SERVES 4

½ cup coarsely chopped fresh cilantro
   leaves and stalks

1½ cups coarsely chopped fresh spinach

1-inch/2.5-cm piece fresh ginger,
   coarsely chopped

3 garlic cloves, coarsely chopped

2–3 fresh green chiles, coarsely chopped

¼ cup fresh mint leaves

1½ tbsp lemon juice

⅓ cup plain yogurt

4 tbsp sunflower oil or olive oil

1 large onion, finely chopped

1 lb 9 oz/700 g skinless chicken thighs
   or breast portions, cut into
   1-inch/2.5-cm cubes

1 tsp ground turmeric

½ tsp sugar

salt

1 small tomato, seeded and cut into
   julienne strips, to garnish

cooked basmati rice, to serve

Place the cilantro, spinach, ginger, garlic, chiles, mint, lemon juice, and ½ teaspoon of salt in a food processor or blender and process to a smooth paste. Add a little water, if necessary, to facilitate blade movement in a blender. Remove and set aside.

Whisk the yogurt until smooth (this is important as the yogurt will curdle otherwise) and set aside. Heat the oil in a medium saucepan and cook the onion for 5–6 minutes, stirring frequently, until softened.

Add the chicken and stir-fry over medium–high heat for 2–3 minutes, until the meat turns opaque. Add the turmeric, sugar, and salt to taste and stir-fry for an additional 2 minutes, then reduce the heat to medium, and add half the yogurt. Cook for 1 minute and add the remaining yogurt, then continue cooking over medium heat until the yogurt resembles a thick batter and the oil is visible.

Add the herb and spice mixture and cook for 4–5 minutes, stirring continuously. Remove from the heat and garnish with the strips of tomato. Serve with cooked basmati rice.

Fried Chile Chicken

This recipe, known as ayam goreng berlada, *is from the fabulous range of light, fragrant, and aromatic dishes cooked in Malaysia. Influenced by India, China, Indonesia, and other neighboring countries, Malaysia today offers a delightful melange of cross-cultural cuisine. This is a simple but superb recipe in which the chicken is cooked in a paste made of just four fresh spices with a light touch of turmeric.*

SERVES 4

1 lb 10 oz/750 g chicken thighs

3 tbsp lemon juice

1 tsp salt, or to taste

5 large garlic cloves, coarsely chopped

2-inch/5-cm piece of fresh ginger, coarsely chopped

1 onion, coarsely chopped

2 fresh red chiles, coarsely chopped

4 tbsp peanut oil

1 tsp ground turmeric

½ tsp chili powder

⅔ cup warm water

3–4 fresh green chiles

cooked basmati rice, to serve

Put the chicken in a nonmetallic bowl and rub in the lemon juice and salt. Set aside for 30 minutes.

Meanwhile, process the garlic, ginger, onion, and red chiles in a food processor or blender. Add a little water, if necessary, to help blade movement in the blender.

Heat the oil in a wide shallow saucepan, preferably nonstick, over medium–high heat. When the oil is hot, cook the chicken in 2 batches, until browned on all sides. Drain on paper towels.

Add the fresh spice paste to the pan with the turmeric and chili powder and reduce the heat to medium. Cook for 5–6 minutes, stirring frequently. Add the chicken and the warm water. Bring to a boil, reduce the heat to low, cover, and cook for 20 minutes. Increase the heat to medium, cover, and cook for a further 8–10 minutes, stirring halfway through to make sure that the thickened sauce does not stick to the bottom of the pan.

Remove the lid and cook until the sauce is reduced to a paste-like consistency, stirring frequently to prevent the sauce from sticking. Add the green chiles, cook for 2–3 minutes, remove from the heat, and serve with cooked basmati rice.

Sri Lankan Chicken Curry

The cuisine of Sri Lanka is not dissimilar to that of southern India, whose key ingredients are coconut milk and tamarind. Sri Lankan cuisine is differentiated from this as it uses its own unique blend of curry powder with spices that are dark roasted and ground to a fine powder. This is a delectable curry with a generous amount of chiles, but the pungency is mellowed by rich coconut milk.

SERVES 4

1 lb 9 oz/700 g skinless, boneless chicken thighs or breast portions

1 tsp salt, or to taste

2 tbsp white wine vinegar

2 tsp coriander seeds

1 tsp cumin seeds

1-inch/2.5-cm piece of cinnamon stick, broken up

4 cloves

4 green cardamom pods

6 fenugreek seeds

4 dried red chiles, torn into pieces

10–12 curry leaves

4 tbsp sunflower oil or olive oil

1 large onion, finely chopped

2 tsp ginger paste

2 tsp garlic paste

1 tsp ground turmeric

½ tsp chili powder

1 lemongrass stalk, thinly sliced

7 oz/200 g canned chopped tomatoes

1 cup coconut cream

cooked basmati rice, to serve

Cut the chicken into 2-inch/5-cm chunks and put them in a bowl. Add the salt and vinegar, mix well, and set aside for 30 minutes.

Preheat a small heavy-bottom saucepan over medium heat and dry-roast the coriander seeds, cumin seeds, cinnamon, cloves, cardamom, fenugreek, chiles, and curry leaves until they are dark, but not black. Remove and let cool, then grind finely in a coffee grinder. Set aside.

Heat the oil in a medium saucepan, add the onion, and cook over medium heat for 5 minutes, until it is translucent. Add the ginger paste and garlic paste and continue to cook for an additional 2 minutes.

Add the turmeric, chili powder, chicken, and the ground spice mix. Stir and mix well, then add the lemongrass, tomatoes, and coconut cream. Bring to a boil, reduce the heat to low, cover the pan, and cook for 30 minutes.

Serve with cooked basmati rice.

Meat

Lamb Pasanda

Here is a legacy from the glorious days of the Mogul courts, when Indian cooking reached a refined peak. The word pasanda, *from which this creamy dish gets its name, indicates small pieces of boneless meat, in this case tender lamb, flattened as thin as possible.*

SERVES 4-6

1 lb 5 oz/600 g boneless shoulder or leg of lamb

2 tbsp garlic and ginger paste

4 tbsp ghee, vegetable oil, or peanut oil

3 large onions, chopped

1 fresh green chile, seeded and chopped

2 green cardamom pods, bruised

1 cinnamon stick, broken in half

2 tsp ground coriander

1 tsp ground cumin

1 tsp ground turmeric

generous 1 cup water

⅔ cup heavy cream

4 tbsp ground almonds

1½ tsp salt

1 tsp garam masala

paprika and toasted slivered almonds, to garnish

Cut the meat into thin slices, then place the slices between plastic wrap and pound with a rolling pin or meat mallet to make them even thinner. Put the lamb slices in a bowl, add the garlic and ginger paste, and use your hands to rub the paste into the lamb. Cover and set aside in a cool place to marinate for 2 hours.

Melt the ghee in a large skillet with a tight-fitting lid over medium–high heat. Add the onions and chile and sauté, stirring frequently, for 5–8 minutes, until the onions are golden brown.

Stir in the cardamom pods, cinnamon stick, coriander, cumin, and turmeric and continue stirring for 2 minutes, or until the spices are aromatic.

Add the meat to the skillet and cook, stirring occasionally, for about 5 minutes, until it is browned on all sides and the fat begins to separate. Stir in the water and bring to a boil, still stirring. Reduce the heat to its lowest setting, cover the skillet tightly, and simmer for 40 minutes, or until the meat is tender.

When the lamb is tender, stir the cream and ground almonds together in a bowl. Beat in 6 tablespoons of the hot cooking liquid from the skillet, then gradually beat this mixture back into the skillet. Stir in the salt and garam masala. Continue to simmer for an additional 5 minutes, uncovered, stirring occasionally.

Garnish with a sprinkling of paprika and toasted slivered almonds and serve.

COOK'S TIP

To toast slivered almonds, put them in a dry skillet over medium heat and stir continuously until golden brown. Immediately turn them out of the skillet because they can burn quickly.

Lamb in Fragrant Spinach Sauce

This robust home-style dish hails from the northern state of the Punjab, where people love good food drenched in homemade butter! Known as saag gosht, *this dish is traditionally eaten with Indian bread, such as naan or paratha, but it tastes equally good with rice.*

SERVES 4

1 lb 9 oz/700 g boneless leg of lamb

⅓ cup Greek-style yogurt

2 tbsp vinegar

2 tsp chickpea flour

1 tsp ground turmeric

4 tbsp sunflower oil or olive oil

2-inch/5-cm piece cinnamon stick, halved

5 cloves

5 green cardamom pods, bruised

2 bay leaves

1 large onion, finely chopped

2 tsp garlic paste

2 tsp ginger paste

2 tsp ground cumin

½–1 tsp chili powder

7 oz/200 g canned chopped tomatoes

¾ cup warm water, plus 4 tbsp

1 tsp salt, or to taste

1 tsp sugar

9 oz/250 g spinach leaves, thawed if frozen, chopped

2 tsp ghee or unsalted butter

1 large garlic clove, finely chopped

¼ tsp freshly grated nutmeg

1 tsp garam masala

½ cup light cream

Indian bread, to serve

Trim the excess fat from the meat and cut into 1-inch/2.5-cm cubes. Put the yogurt in a nonmetallic bowl and beat with a fork or wire whisk until smooth. Add the vinegar, chickpea flour, and turmeric and beat again until well blended. Add the meat and mix thoroughly. Cover and let marinate in the refrigerator for 4–5 hours, or overnight. Return to room temperature before cooking.

Heat the oil in a medium heavy-bottom saucepan over low heat. Add the cinnamon, cloves, cardamom pods, and bay leaves and cook gently, stirring, for 25–30 seconds, then add the onion. Increase the heat to medium and cook, stirring frequently, for 4–5 minutes, until the onion is softened and translucent. Add the garlic and ginger pastes and cook for an additional 5–6 minutes, until the onion is a pale golden color.

Add the cumin and chili powder and cook, stirring, for 1 minute. Add the tomatoes and cook for 5–6 minutes, stirring frequently, then add the 4 tablespoons of warm water. Cook for an additional 3 minutes, or until the oil separates from the spice paste. Add the marinated meat, increase the heat slightly, and cook, stirring, for 5–6 minutes, until the meat changes color. Add the salt and sugar, stir, then pour in ¾ cup of warm water. Bring to a boil, then reduce the heat to low, cover, and simmer, stirring occasionally, for 55–60 minutes.

Meanwhile, blanch the spinach in a large saucepan of boiling water for 2 minutes. Drain and immediately plunge into cold water. Melt the ghee in a separate medium saucepan over low heat. Add the chopped garlic and cook, stirring, until the garlic is lightly browned. Stir in the nutmeg and garam masala. Squeeze out the excess water from the spinach, add to the spiced butter, and stir to mix thoroughly. Add the spinach mixture to the curry, then add the cream. Stir to mix well and simmer, uncovered, for 2–3 minutes. Serve with Indian bread.

Lamb Rogan Josh

Originally from Kashmir, this fragrant rich dish was quickly adopted by Mogul cooks and has remained a firm favorite in northern India ever since. A Kashmiri natural dye called rattanjog *originally provided the characteristic red color, but chili powder and tomato paste provide a more readily available and less expensive alternative in this recipe.*

SERVES 4

1½ cups plain yogurt

½ tsp ground asafetida, dissolved in
  2 tbsp water

1 lb 9 oz/700 g boneless leg of lamb,
  trimmed and cut into 2-inch/5-cm
  cubes

2 tomatoes, seeded and chopped

1 onion, chopped

2 tbsp ghee, vegetable oil, or peanut oil

1½ tbsp garlic and ginger paste

2 tbsp tomato paste

2 bay leaves

1 tbsp ground coriander

¼–1 tsp chili powder, ideally Kashmiri
  chili powder

½ tsp ground turmeric

1 tsp salt

½ tsp garam masala

Put the yogurt in a large bowl and stir in the dissolved asafetida. Add the lamb and use your hands to rub in all the marinade, then set aside for 30 minutes.

Meanwhile, put the tomatoes and onion in a food processor or blender and process until blended. Melt the ghee in a flameproof casserole or large skillet with a tight-fitting lid. Add the garlic and ginger paste and stir until the aromas are released.

Stir in the tomato mixture, tomato paste, bay leaves, coriander, chili powder, and turmeric, reduce the heat to low, and simmer, stirring occasionally, for 5–8 minutes.

Add the lamb and salt with any leftover marinade and stir for 2 minutes. Cover, reduce the heat to low, and simmer, stirring occasionally, for 30 minutes. The lamb should give off enough moisture to prevent it from catching on the bottom of the skillet, but if the sauce looks too dry, stir in a little water.

Sprinkle with the garam masala, re-cover the skillet, and continue simmering for 15–20 minutes, until the lamb is tender. Serve immediately.

COOK'S TIP

For an authentic flavor, search out the bright red Kashmiri chili powder sold in Indian stores.

Lamb Dhansak

For India's numerous Parsis, this rich dish is served for a Sunday family lunch. The lentils and pumpkin dissolve into a velvety smooth sauce, and all that is needed to complete the meal are rice and naans.

SERVES 4-6

1 lb 9 oz/700 g boneless shoulder of
    lamb, trimmed and cut into 2-inch/
    5-cm cubes

1 tbsp garlic and ginger paste

5 green cardamom pods

1 cup yellow lentils (toor dal)

3½ oz/100 g pumpkin, peeled, seeded,
    and chopped

1 carrot, thinly sliced

1 fresh green chile, seeded and chopped

1 tsp fenugreek powder

scant 2½ cups water

1 large onion, thinly sliced

2 tbsp ghee, vegetable oil, or peanut oil

2 garlic cloves, crushed

salt

chopped fresh cilantro,
    to garnish

DHANSAK MASALA

1 tsp garam masala

½ tsp ground coriander

½ tsp ground cumin

½ tsp chili powder

½ tsp ground turmeric

¼ tsp ground cardamom

¼ tsp ground cloves

Put the lamb and 1 teaspoon of salt in a large saucepan with enough water to cover and bring to a boil. Reduce the heat and simmer, skimming the surface as necessary until no more foam rises. Stir in the garlic and ginger paste and cardamom pods and continue simmering for a total of 30 minutes.

Meanwhile, put the lentils, pumpkin, carrot, chile, and fenugreek powder in a large heavy-bottom saucepan and pour over the water. Bring to a boil, stirring occasionally, then reduce the heat and simmer for 20–30 minutes, until the lentils and carrot are very tender. Stir in a little extra water if the lentils look as though they will catch on the bottom of the pan.

Let the lentil mixture cool slightly, then pour it into a food processor or blender and process until a thick, smooth sauce forms.

While the lamb and lentils are cooking, put the onion in a bowl, sprinkle with 1 teaspoon of salt, and let stand for about 5 minutes to extract the moisture. Use your hands to squeeze out the moisture.

Melt the ghee in a flameproof casserole or large skillet with a tight-fitting lid over high heat. Add the onion and sauté, stirring, for 2 minutes. Remove one third of the onion and continue sautéing the rest for an additional 1–2 minutes, until golden brown. Immediately take a slotted spoon and remove the remaining onion, as it will continue to darken as it cools.

Return the reserved onion to the casserole with the garlic. Stir in all the dhansak masala ingredients and cook for 2 minutes, stirring continuously. Add the cooked lamb and stir for an additional 2 minutes. Add the lentil sauce and simmer over medium heat to warm through, stirring and adding a little extra water, if needed. Adjust the seasoning, if necessary. Sprinkle with the remaining onion and garnish with cilantro.

Lamb Shanks Marathani

From Mumbai, this dish is bursting with lots of flavors that reflect the city's vibrancy and diversity. It's not for nothing that the port city is known as "The Gateway to India," as traders from all corners of the globe have always sold their wares here. Marathani *in a recipe title indicates that a dish comes from the state of Maharashtra, of which Mumbai is the capital.*

SERVES 4

4 tbsp ghee, vegetable oil, or peanut oil

2 large onions, thinly sliced

generous ¼ cup cashew nuts

1½ tbsp garlic and ginger paste

2 fresh green chiles, seeded and
  chopped

2 cinnamon sticks, broken in half

½ tsp chili powder

½ tsp ground turmeric

½ tsp ground coriander

¼ tsp ground mace

3 tbsp plain yogurt

4 lamb shanks

3½ cups water

½ tsp garam masala

salt and pepper

chopped fresh cilantro, to garnish

cooked basmati rice, to serve

Melt half the ghee in a large flameproof casserole over medium–high heat. Add the onions and sauté, stirring frequently, for 5–8 minutes, until softened but not browned. Stir in the cashew nuts and stir around for just 1–2 minutes, until they turn light brown.

Use a slotted spoon to remove the onions and nuts from the casserole and let cool slightly. Transfer both to a food processor or mortar and grind to a paste.

Melt the remaining ghee in the casserole. Add the garlic and ginger paste, chiles, and cinnamon sticks and stir for about 1 minute, until you can smell the aromas.

Stir in the chili powder, turmeric, coriander, and mace. Gradually stir in the yogurt, stirring continuously. Add the lamb shanks and continue stirring for about 5 minutes, until the yogurt is absorbed.

Stir in the reserved onion and cashew paste. Pour in enough of the water to cover the lamb shanks, add the garam masala, and bring to a boil. Reduce the heat to low, cover the casserole, and let simmer for 1¾–2 hours, until the lamb is very tender and almost falling off the bones.

Taste and adjust the seasoning, if necessary. Transfer the lamb shanks to a serving dish and spoon over the thin sauce. Garnish with chopped cilantro and serve with cooked basmati rice.

Lamb in Cinnamon-Scented Fenugreek Sauce

This lovely north Indian dish bursts with the flavors of powerful fenugreek, pungent chiles, aromatic cloves, and sweet cinnamon. The lamb is marinated in red wine vinegar, ginger, and garlic, and gentle, prolonged cooking enables the meat to absorb all the wonderful flavors.

SERVES 4

1 lb 9 oz/700 g boneless leg or shoulder
  of lamb, cut into 1-inch/2.5-cm cubes

4 tbsp red wine vinegar

1 tsp salt, or to taste

4 tbsp sunflower oil or olive oil

2-inch/5-cm piece cinnamon stick,
  halved

5 green cardamom pods, bruised

5 cloves

1 large onion, finely chopped

2 tsp ginger paste

2 tsp garlic paste

2 tsp ground cumin

1 tsp ground turmeric

½–1 tsp chili powder

8 oz/225 g canned chopped tomatoes

1½ tbsp dried fenugreek leaves

¾ cup warm water

2 tsp ghee or unsalted butter

½ tsp garam masala

fresh cilantro sprigs, to garnish

Indian bread or cooked basmati rice,
  to serve

Put the meat in a nonmetallic bowl and rub in the vinegar and salt. Set aside for 30–40 minutes.

Heat the oil in a medium heavy-bottom saucepan over low heat and add the cinnamon, cardamom, and cloves. Let them sizzle for 25–30 seconds, then add the onion, increase the heat to medium, and cook, stirring frequently, until the onion is softened but not browned.

Add the ginger and garlic pastes and cook for an additional 2–3 minutes, then add the cumin, turmeric, and chili powder. Cook for 1–2 minutes and add the tomatoes. Increase the heat slightly and continue to cook until the tomatoes are reduced to a paste-like consistency and the oil separates from the paste. Reduce the heat toward the last 2–3 minutes.

Add the meat, fenugreek leaves, and the warm water. Bring to a boil, reduce the heat to low, cover, and simmer for 45–50 minutes, or until the meat is tender.

In a small saucepan melt the ghee over low heat and stir in the garam masala. Cook for 30 seconds, then fold the spiced ghee into the curry. Remove from the heat, garnish with cilantro sprigs, and serve with some Indian bread.

Peshawar-Style Lamb Curry

Peshawar, in the Northwest Frontier Province, was created during the British Raj to safeguard India from foreign invaders. The cuisine of this area is famous for its robust flavors and brilliant colors. This lamb curry is in a class of its own.

SERVES 4

4 tbsp sunflower oil or olive oil

1-inch/2.5-cm piece cinnamon stick

5 green cardamom pods, bruised

5 cloves

2 bay leaves

1 lb 9 oz/700 g boneless leg of lamb, cut into 1-inch/2.5-cm cubes

1 large onion, finely chopped

2 tsp ginger paste

2 tsp garlic paste

1 tbsp tomato paste

1 tsp ground turmeric

1 tsp ground coriander

1 tsp ground cumin

generous ½ cup thick plain yogurt

2 tsp chickpea flour or cornstarch

½–1 tsp chili powder

⅔ cup warm water

1 tbsp chopped fresh mint leaves

2 tbsp chopped fresh cilantro leaves

Indian bread, to serve

In a medium saucepan, heat the oil over low heat and add the cinnamon, cardamom, cloves, and bay leaves. Let them sizzle for 25–30 seconds, then add the meat, increase the heat to medium–high, and cook until the meat begins to brown and all the natural juices have evaporated.

Add the onion, garlic paste, and ginger paste and cook for 5–6 minutes, stirring frequently, then add the tomato paste, turmeric, coriander, and cumin. Continue to cook for 3–4 minutes.

Whisk together the yogurt, chickpea flour, and chili powder and add to the meat. Reduce the heat to low, add the warm water, cover, and simmer, stirring frequently to make sure that the sauce does not stick to the bottom of the pan, for 45–50 minutes, until the meat is tender. Simmer, uncovered, if necessary to thicken the sauce to the desired consistency.

Stir in the fresh mint and cilantro, remove from the heat, and serve with Indian bread.

Kheema Matar

When the cold winter winds come to northern India, this simple, rustic dish makes a popular family meal.

SERVES 4-6

2 tbsp ghee, vegetable oil, or peanut oil

2 tsp cumin seeds

1 large onion, finely chopped

1 tbsp garlic and ginger paste

2 bay leaves

1 tsp mild, medium, or hot curry
    powder, to taste

2 tomatoes, seeded and chopped

1 tsp ground coriander

¼–½ tsp chili powder

¼ tsp ground turmeric

pinch of sugar

½ teaspoon salt

½ teaspoon pepper

1 lb 2 oz/500 g lean ground beef
    or lamb

2¼ cups frozen peas, straight from
    the freezer

Melt the ghee in a flameproof casserole or large skillet with a tight-fitting lid. Add the cumin seeds and cook, stirring, for 30 seconds, or until they start to crackle.

Stir in the onion, garlic and ginger paste, bay leaves, and curry powder and continue to stir-fry until the fat separates.

Stir in the tomatoes and cook for 1–2 minutes. Stir in the coriander, chili powder, turmeric, sugar, salt, and pepper and stir around for 30 seconds.

Add the beef and cook for 5 minutes, or until it is no longer pink, using a wooden spoon to break up the meat. Reduce the heat and simmer, stirring occasionally, for 10 minutes.

Add the peas and continue simmering for an additional 10–15 minutes, until the peas are thawed and hot. If there is too much liquid left in the casserole, increase the heat and let it bubble for a few minutes until it reduces.

Beef Madras

This spicy curry with a hint of coconut gets its Indian name from the southeastern coastal town of Chennai, formerly known as Madras. The regional specialties are typically flavored with coconut and lots of chiles, which is why restaurant menus frequently label every hot dish as "madras."

SERVES 4–6

1–2 dried red chiles

2 tsp ground coriander

2 tsp ground turmeric

1 tsp black mustard seeds

½ tsp ground ginger

¼ tsp pepper

1¼ cups coconut cream

4 tbsp ghee, vegetable oil, or peanut oil

2 onions, chopped

3 large garlic cloves, chopped

1 lb 9 oz/700 g lean braising beef, trimmed and cut into 2-inch/5-cm cubes

generous 1 cup beef stock, plus a little extra if necessary

lemon juice

salt

Depending on how hot you want this dish to be, chop the chiles with or without any seeds. The more seeds you include, the hotter the dish will be. Put the chopped chiles and any seeds in a small bowl with the coriander, turmeric, mustard seeds, ginger, and pepper and stir in a little of the coconut cream to make a thin paste.

Melt the ghee in a flameproof casserole or large skillet with a tight-fitting lid over medium–high heat. Add the onions and garlic and cook for 5–8 minutes, stirring frequently, until the onion is golden brown. Add the spice paste and stir for 2 minutes, or until you can smell the aromas.

Add the meat and stock and bring to a boil. Reduce the heat to its lowest level, cover tightly, and simmer for 1½ hours, or until the beef is tender. Check occasionally that the meat isn't catching on the bottom of the casserole, and stir in a little extra water or stock, if necessary.

Uncover the casserole and stir in the remaining coconut cream with the lemon juice and salt to taste. Bring to a boil, stirring, then reduce the heat again and simmer, still uncovered, until the sauce reduces slightly.

COOK'S TIP

The dish takes on a different character, but is equally flavorsome, if you omit the chiles altogether and garnish with toasted flaked coconut just before serving.

Balti Beef

Direct from Birmingham, England, this is the Indian/Pakistani version of stir-frying. Immigrants introduced "Brummies" to this quick style of cooking and now balti restaurants thrive throughout the UK and Europe. It's quick cooking once you've made the balti sauce, but that can be made in advance and refrigerated for several days.

SERVES 4-6

2 tbsp ghee, vegetable oil, or peanut oil

1 large onion, chopped

2 garlic cloves, crushed

2 large red bell peppers, seeded and chopped

1 lb 5 oz/600 g boneless beef, such as sirloin, thinly sliced

fresh cilantro sprigs, to garnish

Indian bread, to serve

BALTI SAUCE

2 tbsp ghee, vegetable oil, or peanut oil

2 large onions, chopped

1 tbsp garlic and ginger paste

14 oz/400 g canned chopped tomatoes

1 tsp ground paprika

½ tsp ground turmeric

½ tsp ground cumin

½ tsp ground coriander

¼ tsp chili powder

¼ tsp ground cardamom

1 bay leaf

salt and pepper

To make the balti sauce, melt the ghee in a wok or large skillet over medium–high heat. Add the onions and garlic and ginger paste and stir-fry for about 5 minutes, until the onions are golden brown. Stir in the tomatoes, then add the paprika, turmeric, cumin, coriander, chili powder, cardamom, bay leaf, and salt and pepper to taste. Bring to a boil, stirring, then reduce the heat and simmer for 20 minutes, stirring occasionally.

Let the sauce cool slightly, then remove the bay leaf and pour the mixture into a food processor or blender and process to a smooth sauce.

Wipe out the wok and return it to medium–high heat. Add the ghee and melt. Add the onion and garlic and stir-fry for 5–8 minutes, until golden brown. Add the bell peppers and continue stir-frying for 2 minutes.

Stir in the beef and continue stirring for 2 minutes, until it starts to turn brown. Add the balti sauce and bring to a boil. Reduce the heat and simmer for 5 minutes, or until the sauce slightly reduces again and the bell peppers are tender. Adjust the seasoning, if necessary. Garnish with cilantro sprigs and serve with Indian bread.

Coconut Beef Curry

This rich and aromatic curry uses Mussaman curry paste, which is a Thai curry paste with Islamic origins. It is unusual because it contains a number of spices that are more common in Indian cuisine than in Thai, such as cloves, cardamom, coriander, and cumin.

SERVES 4

1 tbsp ground coriander

1 tbsp ground cumin

3 tbsp Mussaman curry paste

scant 1 cup coconut cream

1 lb/450 g beef tenderloin, cut into strips

1¾ cups coconut milk

½ cup unsalted peanuts, finely chopped

2 tbsp fish sauce

1 tsp jaggery or light brown sugar

4 kaffir lime leaves

fresh cilantro sprigs, to garnish

cooked rice, to serve

Combine the coriander, cumin, and curry paste in a bowl. Pour the coconut cream into a saucepan and bring just to a boil. Add the curry paste mixture and let simmer for 1 minute.

Add the beef and let simmer for 6–8 minutes, then add the coconut milk, peanuts, fish sauce, and jaggery. Let simmer gently for 15–20 minutes, until the meat is tender.

Add the lime leaves and let simmer for 1–2 minutes. Garnish with cilantro sprigs and serve with cooked rice.

Beef Rendang

Prime-quality beef is essential to make a good rendang. Although other meats, such as chicken, lamb, and pork, are also used, beef is by far the best choice in a traditional rendang, which is enjoyed all over Indonesia with plain boiled rice. The quantity of chiles may seem excessive, but the pungency is mellowed by the two different ways in which the coconut is used.

SERVES 4

5–6 dried red chiles

2–3 fresh red chiles, coarsely chopped

4–5 shallots or 1 large onion, coarsely
   chopped

4 large garlic cloves, coarsely chopped

1-inch/2.5-cm piece fresh ginger,
   coarsely chopped

2 tbsp water

1 tsp coriander seeds

1 tsp cumin seeds

⅔ cup dry unsweetened coconut

4 tbsp peanut oil

1 lb 9 oz/700 g prime-quality braising
   beef, trimmed and cut into
   1-inch/2.5-cm cubes

1 tbsp dark soy sauce

1 lemongrass stalk, finely chopped

3 kaffir lime leaves, shredded

½ tsp salt

scant 1 cup warm water

1 tbsp tamarind juice

1¾ cups coconut milk

toasted shredded coconut, to garnish

cooked rice, to serve

Soak the dried chiles in boiling water for 10 minutes, then drain and place in a food processor or blender. Add the fresh chiles, shallots, garlic, ginger, and the 2 tablespoons of water and process until the mixture is smooth.

Preheat a small heavy saucepan over medium heat and add the coriander and cumin seeds. Stir for about a minute until they release their aroma, remove them from the pan, and let cool. In the same pan, dry-roast the dry unsweetened coconut, stirring continuously, until it is tinged with a light brown color. Remove and let cool, then mix the coconut with the roasted spices, and grind in 2 batches in a coffee grinder.

Heat the oil in a medium saucepan and add the processed ingredients. Cook over medium heat, stirring frequently, for 5–6 minutes. Add a little water to prevent the mixture from sticking, if necessary, and continue to cook for an additional 5–6 minutes, adding water if necessary.

Add the meat and increase the heat to medium–high, stir until the meat changes color, and add the roasted coconut mixture, soy sauce, lemongrass, lime leaves, and salt. Stir and mix well and pour in the warm water. Bring to a boil, reduce the heat to low, cover, and simmer for 45 minutes, stirring occasionally to make sure that the mixture does not stick to the bottom of the pan.

Add the tamarind juice and coconut milk, bring to a gentle simmer, cover, and cook for an additional 45 minutes, or until the meat is tender. Remove the lid and cook over medium heat, if necessary to thicken the sauce. Garnish with the toasted coconut and serve with cooked rice.

Mussaman Curry

A very traditional dish that combines potatoes and peanuts with beef tenderloin, and tastes fantastic!

SERVES 4

2 tbsp peanut oil or vegetable oil

8 oz/225 g shallots, coarsely chopped

1 garlic clove, crushed

1 lb/450 g beef tenderloin, thickly sliced and then cut into 1-inch/ 2.5-cm cubes

2 tbsp Mussaman curry paste

3 potatoes, cut into 1-inch/2.5-cm cubes

1¾ cups coconut milk

2 tbsp soy sauce

⅔ cup beef stock

1 tsp jaggery or light brown sugar

½ cup unsalted peanuts

handful of fresh cilantro, chopped

noodles or cooked rice, to serve

Heat the oil in a preheated wok. Add the shallots and garlic and stir-fry over medium–high heat for 1–2 minutes, or until softened. Add the beef and curry paste and stir-fry over high heat for 2–3 minutes, or until browned all over. Add the potatoes, coconut milk, soy sauce, stock, and jaggery and bring gently to a boil, stirring occasionally. Reduce the heat and simmer for 8–10 minutes, or until the potatoes are tender.

Meanwhile, heat a dry skillet until hot, then add the peanuts and cook over medium–high heat, shaking the skillet frequently, for 2–3 minutes, or until lightly browned. Add to the curry with the cilantro and stir well. Serve hot with noodles or cooked rice.

COOK'S TIP

To help the skins of the shallots come off more easily, put them in a heatproof bowl and cover with boiling water, then let stand for 10 minutes.

Pork Vindaloo

The name vindaloo *is derived from two Portuguese words:* vin, *meaning "vinegar," and* alho, *meaning "garlic." When the Portuguese traveled to India, they took pork preserved in vinegar, garlic, and pepper, which was spiced up to suit Indian tastes!*

SERVES 4

2–6 dried red chiles (long slim variety),
   torn into 2 or 3 pieces
5 cloves
1-inch/2.5-cm piece cinnamon stick,
   broken up
4 green cardamom pods
½ tsp black peppercorns
½ mace blade
¼ nutmeg, lightly crushed
1 tsp cumin seeds
1½ tsp coriander seeds
½ tsp fenugreek seeds
2 tsp garlic paste
1 tbsp ginger paste
3 tbsp cider vinegar or white wine
   vinegar
1 tbsp tamarind juice or juice of ½ lime
1 lb 9 oz/700 g boneless leg of pork,
   cut into 1-inch/2.5-cm cubes
4 tbsp sunflower oil or olive oil,
   plus 2 tsp
2 large onions, finely chopped
generous 1 cup warm water, plus 4 tbsp
1 tsp salt, or to taste
1 tsp dark brown sugar
2 large garlic cloves, finely sliced
8–10 fresh or dried curry leaves
cooked basmati rice, to serve

Grind the first ten ingredients (all the spices) to a fine powder in a coffee grinder. Transfer the ground spices to a bowl and add the garlic and ginger pastes, vinegar, and tamarind juice. Mix together to form a paste.

Put the pork in a large nonmetallic bowl and rub about one quarter of the spice paste into the meat. Cover and let marinate in the refrigerator for 30–40 minutes.

Heat the 4 tablespoons of oil in a medium heavy-bottom saucepan over medium heat, add the onions, and cook, stirring frequently, for 8–10 minutes, until lightly browned. Add the remaining spice paste and cook, stirring continuously, for 5–6 minutes. Add 2 tablespoons of the warm water and cook until it evaporates. Repeat with the other 2 tablespoons of warm water.

Add the marinated pork and cook over medium–high heat for 5–6 minutes, until the meat changes color. Add the salt, sugar, and 1 cup of warm water. Bring to a boil, then reduce the heat to low, cover, and simmer for 50–55 minutes, until the meat is tender.

Meanwhile, heat the 2 teaspoons of oil in a very small saucepan over low heat. Add the sliced garlic and cook, stirring frequently, until it begins to brown. Add the curry leaves and let sizzle for 15–20 seconds. Stir the garlic mixture into the vindaloo. Remove from the heat and serve immediately with cooked basmati rice.

Railroad Pork & Vegetables

East meets West in the Christian Anglo-Indian kitchens of Kolkata, where the tradition of flavoring British-style dishes with Indian ingredients lives on. This example is an updated version of the railroad curries once served in dining cars.

SERVES 4-6

3 tbsp ghee, vegetable oil, or peanut oil

1 large onion, finely chopped

4 green cardamom pods

3 cloves

1 cinnamon stick

1 tbsp garlic and ginger paste

2 tsp garam masala

¼–½ tsp chili powder

½ tsp ground asafetida

2 tsp salt

1 lb 5 oz/600 g lean ground pork

1 potato, scrubbed and cut into
    ¼-inch/5-mm dice

14 oz/400 g canned chopped tomatoes

½ cup water

1 bay leaf

1 large carrot, coarsely grated

Melt the ghee in a flameproof casserole or large skillet with a tight-fitting lid over medium heat. Add the onion and sauté, stirring occasionally, for 5–8 minutes, until golden brown. Add the cardamom pods, cloves, and cinnamon stick and continue sautéing, stirring, for 1 minute, or until you can smell the aromas.

Add the garlic and ginger paste, garam masala, chili powder, asafetida, and salt and stir for an additional minute. Add the pork and cook for 5 minutes, or until no longer pink, using a wooden spoon to break up the meat.

Add the potato, tomatoes, water, and bay leaf and bring to a boil, stirring. Reduce the heat to the lowest level, cover tightly, and simmer for 15 minutes. Stir in the carrot and simmer for an additional 5 minutes, or until the potato and carrot are tender. Taste and adjust the seasoning, if necessary, and serve.

COOK'S TIP

Lean ground lamb or beef can be used instead of the pork.

Red Curry Pork with Bell Peppers

This dish is a delightful combination of succulent pork, tender mushrooms and sweet bell peppers. The mushrooms act like little sponges, soaking up the fragrant coconut sauce beautifully.

SERVES 4

2 tbsp vegetable oil or peanut oil

1 onion, coarsely chopped

2 garlic cloves, chopped

1 lb/450 g pork tenderloin, thickly sliced

1 red bell pepper, seeded and cut into squares

6 oz/175 g button mushrooms, quartered

2 tbsp Thai red curry paste

2½ cups coconut cream

1 tsp pork or vegetable bouillon powder

2 tbsp Thai soy sauce

4 tomatoes, peeled, seeded, and chopped

handful of fresh cilantro, chopped, plus extra to garnish

cooked rice noodles, to serve

Heat the oil in a wok or large skillet and sauté the onion and garlic for 1–2 minutes, until they are softened but not browned.

Add the pork slices and stir-fry for 2–3 minutes, until browned all over. Add the bell pepper, mushrooms, and curry paste.

Add the coconut cream to the wok with the bouillon powder and soy sauce. Bring to a boil and let simmer for 4–5 minutes, until the liquid has reduced and thickened.

Add the tomatoes and cilantro and cook for 1–2 minutes. Garnish with extra chopped coriander and serve with cooked rice noodles.

Pork with Mixed Green Beans

Quick and convenient, this tasty Thai-style pork curry uses a mixture of different beans—green beans, fava beans, and string beans—and covers them in a spicy sauce enriched with peanuts.

SERVES 4

2 tbsp vegetable oil or peanut oil

2 shallots, chopped

8 oz/225 g pork tenderloin, thinly sliced

1-inch/2.5-cm piece fresh galangal, thinly sliced

2 garlic cloves, chopped

1¼ cups chicken stock

4 tbsp chili sauce

4 tbsp crunchy peanut butter

4 oz/115 g fine green beans, trimmed

generous 1 cup frozen fava beans

4 oz/115 g string beans, trimmed and sliced

crispy noodles, to serve

Heat the oil in a wok and stir-fry the shallots, pork, galangal, and garlic until lightly browned.

Add the stock, chili sauce, and peanut butter, and stir until the peanut butter has melted. Add all the beans and let simmer for 3–4 minutes. Serve hot with crispy noodles.

Pork with Cinnamon & Fenugreek

This is a dry dish, that is one served without an integral sauce. Fenugreek is an aromatic, pungent herb and both the leaves and seeds are used in Asian cooking. It is a common ingredient in curry powders but should be used sparingly because it can be overpowering.

SERVES 4

1 tsp ground coriander

1 tsp ground cumin

1 tsp chili powder

1 tbsp dried fenugreek leaves

1 tsp ground fenugreek

⅔ cup plain yogurt

1 lb/450 g diced pork tenderloin

4 tbsp ghee or vegetable oil

1 large onion, sliced

2-inch/5-cm piece fresh ginger, finely chopped

4 garlic cloves, finely chopped

1 cinnamon stick

6 green cardamom pods

6 whole cloves

2 bay leaves

¾ cup water

salt

Mix the coriander, cumin, chili powder, dried fenugreek, ground fenugreek, and yogurt together in a small bowl. Place the pork in a large, shallow nonmetallic dish and add the spice mixture, turning well to coat. Cover with plastic wrap and let marinate in the refrigerator for 30 minutes.

Melt the ghee in a large heavy-bottom saucepan. Cook the onion over low heat, stirring occasionally, for 5 minutes, or until softened. Add the ginger, garlic, cinnamon stick, cardamom pods, cloves, and bay leaves and cook, stirring continuously, for 2 minutes, or until the spices give off their aroma. Add the meat with its marinade and the water, and season to taste with salt. Bring to a boil, reduce the heat, cover, and let simmer for 30 minutes.

Transfer the meat mixture to a preheated wok or large heavy-bottom skillet and cook over low heat, stirring continuously, until dry and tender. If necessary, sprinkle occasionally with a little water to prevent the mixture from sticking to the wok. Serve immediately.

COOK'S TIP
This recipe would also work well with lean lamb or beef sirloin instead of the pork, if you prefer.

Burmese Pork Curry

The predominant flavor in this curry comes from a very generous quantity of garlic and ginger, which is also a way in which the Burmese preserve their meat. In Burma, vinegar is used for flavoring as well as for preservation. In this recipe, however, dry white wine has been used, which tenderizes the meat beautifully and also acts as a preservative.

SERVES 4

1 lb 9 oz/700 g boneless leg of pork, fat trimmed and cut into 1-inch/2.5-cm cubes

2 tbsp dry white wine

1 tsp salt, or to taste

8 large garlic cloves, coarsely chopped

2-inch/5-cm piece fresh ginger, coarsely chopped

2 fresh red chiles, coarsely chopped

1 large onion, coarsely chopped

1 tsp ground turmeric

½–1 tsp chili powder

3 tbsp peanut oil

1 tbsp sesame oil

scant 1 cup warm water

1 fresh green chile, seeded and cut into julienne strips, to garnish

cooked basmati rice, to serve

Combine the meat, wine, and salt in a nonmetallic bowl and set aside for 1 hour.

Put the garlic, ginger, red chiles, and onion in a food processor or blender and process until the ingredients are mushy. Transfer to a bowl and stir in the turmeric and chili powder.

Heat both types of oil in a medium heavy-bottom saucepan over medium heat and add the processed ingredients. Stir and cook for 5–6 minutes, reduce the heat to low, and continue to cook for an additional 8–10 minutes, occasionally sprinkling over a little water to prevent the spices from sticking to the bottom of the pan.

Add the marinated pork, increase the heat to medium–high, and stir until the meat changes color. Pour in the warm water and bring to a boil, reduce the heat to low, cover, and cook for 1 hour 10 minutes, stirring several times during the last 15–20 minutes to prevent the thickened sauce from sticking. Remove from the heat and garnish with the strips of chile. Serve with cooked basmati rice.

Meatballs in Creamy Cashew Nut Sauce

Known as rista, *this delectable recipe comes from Kashmir, the northernmost state in India, which has a rich culinary heritage. Kashmiri cooking is a work of art and the chefs of this beautiful Himalayan state are extremely skilled as well as creative.*

SERVES 4

generous 1 cup raw cashews

⅔ cup boiling water

1 lb/450 g fresh lean ground lamb

1 tbsp thick plain yogurt

1 large egg, beaten

½ tsp ground cardamom

½ tsp ground nutmeg

½ tsp pepper

½ tsp dried mint

½ tsp salt, or to taste

1¼ cups water

1-inch/2.5-cm piece cinnamon stick

5 green cardamom pods

5 cloves

2 bay leaves

3 tbsp sunflower oil or olive oil

1 onion, finely chopped

2 tsp garlic paste

1 tsp ground ginger

1 tsp ground fennel seeds

½ tsp ground turmeric

½–1 tsp chili powder

⅔ cup heavy cream

1 tbsp crushed pistachios, to garnish

Indian bread or cooked rice, to serve

Soak the cashews in the boiling water for 20 minutes.

Put the lamb into a bowl and add the yogurt, egg, cardamom, nutmeg, pepper, mint, and salt. Knead the meat until it is smooth and velvety. Alternatively, put the ingredients in a food processor and process until fine. Chill the mixture for 30–40 minutes, then divide it into quarters. Make five balls (koftas) out of each quarter and compress so that they are firm, rolling them between your palms to make them smooth and neat.

Bring the cold water to a boil in a large shallow saucepan and add all the whole spices and the bay leaves. Arrange the meatballs in a single layer in the spiced liquid, reduce the heat to medium, cover the pan, and cook for 12–15 minutes.

Remove the meatballs, cover, and keep hot. Strain the spiced stock and set aside.

Wipe out the pan and add the oil. Place over medium heat and add the onion and garlic paste. Cook until the mixture begins to brown and add the ground ginger, fennel, turmeric, and chili powder. Stir-fry for 2–3 minutes, then add the strained stock and meatballs. Bring to a boil, reduce the heat to low, cover, and simmer for 10–12 minutes.

Meanwhile, process the cashews to a paste in a blender and add to the meatball mixture along with the cream. Simmer for an additional 5–6 minutes, then remove from the heat. Garnish with crushed pistachios and serve with Indian bread.

Fish & Seafood

Goan Fish Curry

Goa is well known for its fish and shellfish dishes, which are usually cooked in coconut milk. For this dish, salmon has been chosen because its firm flesh lends itself well to curry dishes and takes on the flavors of all the spices.

SERVES 4

4 skinless salmon fillets,
    about 7 oz/200 g each

1 tsp salt, or to taste

1 tbsp lemon juice

3 tbsp sunflower oil or olive oil

1 large onion, finely chopped

2 tsp garlic paste

2 tsp ginger paste

½ tsp ground turmeric

1 tsp ground coriander

½ tsp ground cumin

½–1 tsp chili powder

generous 1 cup coconut milk

2–3 fresh green chiles, sliced lengthwise
    (seeded if you like)

2 tbsp cider vinegar or white wine
    vinegar

2 tbsp chopped fresh cilantro leaves

cooked basmati rice, to serve

Cut each salmon fillet in half and lay the fish on a flat surface in a single layer. Sprinkle with half the salt and the lemon juice and rub in gently. Cover and let marinate in the refrigerator for 15–20 minutes.

Heat the oil in a skillet over medium heat, add the onion, and cook, stirring frequently to ensure even coloring, for 8–9 minutes, until a pale golden color.

Add the garlic and ginger pastes and cook, stirring, for 1 minute, then add the turmeric, coriander, cumin, and chili powder and cook, stirring, for 1 minute. Add the coconut milk, chiles, and vinegar, and the remaining salt. Stir well, and simmer, uncovered, for 6–8 minutes.

Add the fish and cook gently for 5–6 minutes. Stir in the fresh cilantro and remove from the heat. Serve immediately with cooked basmati rice.

COOK'S TIP

This curry improves in flavor if you cook it in advance and reheat very gently before serving. You can safely store it in the refrigerator for up to 48 hours.

Thai Fish Curry

The beauty of this curry is in the mouthwatering combination of whitefish and oily fish, both of which are extremely beneficial for the health. Make sure you serve this dish with plenty of fragrant jasmine rice to soak up the delicious juices.

SERVES 4

juice of 1 lime

4 tbsp fish sauce

2 tbsp Thai soy sauce

1 fresh red chile, seeded and chopped

12 oz/350 g monkfish fillet, cut into cubes

12 oz/350 g salmon fillet, skinned and cut into cubes

1¾ cups coconut milk

3 kaffir lime leaves

1 tbsp Thai red curry paste

1 lemongrass stalk (white part only), finely chopped

cooked jasmine rice with chopped fresh cilantro, to serve

Combine the lime juice, half the fish sauce, and the soy sauce in a shallow nonmetallic dish. Add the chile and the fish, stir to coat, cover with plastic wrap, and chill for 1–2 hours, or overnight.

Bring the coconut milk to a boil in a saucepan and add the lime leaves, curry paste, the remaining fish sauce, and the lemongrass. Let simmer gently for 10–15 minutes.

Add the fish with its marinade and let simmer for 4–5 minutes, until the fish is cooked. Serve hot, accompanied by cooked jasmine rice with chopped cilantro stirred through it.

Balti Fish Curry

This is for those who prefer robustly flavored dishes, more like the ones served in northern India than the coconut-based ones from the south.

SERVES 4-6

2 lb/900 g thick whitefish fillets, rinsed
    and cut into large chunks

2 bay leaves, torn

5 oz/140 g ghee or ⅔ cup vegetable oil
    or peanut oil

2 large onions, chopped

½ tbsp salt

⅔ cup water

chopped fresh cilantro, to garnish

Indian bread, to serve

MARINADE

½ tbsp garlic and ginger paste

1 fresh green chile, seeded and chopped

1 tsp ground coriander

1 tsp ground cumin

½ tsp ground turmeric

¼–½ tsp chili powder

1 tbsp water

salt

To make the marinade, mix the garlic and ginger paste, chile, coriander, cumin, turmeric, and chili powder together with salt to taste in a large bowl. Gradually stir in the water to form a thin paste. Add the fish chunks and smear with the marinade. Tuck the bay leaves underneath, cover, and let marinate in the refrigerator for at least 30 minutes, or up to 4 hours.

When you are ready to cook the fish, remove from the refrigerator 15 minutes in advance. Melt the ghee in a wok or large skillet over medium–high heat. Add the onions, sprinkle with the salt, and sauté, stirring frequently, for 8 minutes, or until they are very soft and golden.

Gently add the fish with its marinade and the bay leaves to the wok and stir in the water. Bring to a boil, then immediately reduce the heat and cook the fish for 4–5 minutes, spooning the sauce over the fish and carefully moving the chunks around, until they are cooked through and the flesh flakes easily. Garnish with cilantro and serve with Indian bread.

COOK'S TIP

Do not over-brown the onions or the dish will taste bitter. They should be golden, but not browned, when the fish is added.

Thai Green Fish Curry

The warm waters of Thailand's coastal regions are a rich source of fish and seafood. Whitefish is a popular addition to many curries as it soaks up the flavors of the sauce and cooks in no time at all.

SERVES 4

2 tbsp vegetable oil

1 garlic clove, chopped

2 tbsp Thai green curry paste

1 small eggplant, diced

4 fl oz/120 ml coconut cream

2 tbsp fish sauce

1 tsp sugar

8 oz/225 g firm whitefish, cut into pieces

4 fl oz/120 ml fish stock

2 kaffir lime leaves, finely shredded

about 15 fresh Thai basil leaves

fresh dill sprigs, to garnish

Heat the oil in a large skillet or preheated wok over medium heat until almost smoking. Add the garlic and fry until golden. Add the curry paste and stir-fry for a few seconds before adding the eggplant. Stir-fry for about 4–5 minutes, until softened.

Add the coconut cream, bring to a boil, and stir until the cream thickens and curdles slightly. Add the fish sauce and sugar to the skillet and stir well.

Add the fish pieces and stock. Simmer for 3–4 minutes, stirring occasionally, until the fish is just tender. Add the lime leaves and basil, then cook for an additional minute. Transfer to a large, warmed serving dish and garnish with dill sprigs. Serve immediately.

Bengali-Style Fish

Fresh fish is eaten a great deal in Bengal (Bangladesh) and this dish is made with mustard oil, which gives the fish a mouthwatering flavor. The mustard plant flourishes in the hot and humid eastern plains surrounding Bengal, and the resulting oil and seeds are used extensively in Asian cooking.

SERVES 4–8

1 tsp ground turmeric

1 tsp salt

6 tbsp mustard oil

2 lb 4 oz/1 kg whitefish fillets, skinned and cut into pieces

4 fresh green chiles

1 tsp finely chopped fresh ginger

1 tsp crushed garlic

2 onions, finely chopped

2 tomatoes, finely chopped

2 cups water

chopped fresh cilantro, to garnish

Indian bread, to serve

Mix the turmeric and salt together in a small bowl, then spoon the mixture over the fish pieces.

Heat the oil in a large heavy-bottom skillet. Add the fish and cook until pale yellow. Remove the fish with a slotted spoon and set aside.

Place the chiles, ginger, garlic, onions, and tomatoes in a mortar and grind with a pestle to make a paste. Alternatively, place the ingredients in a food processor and process until smooth.

Transfer the spice paste to a clean skillet and dry-fry until golden brown.

Remove the skillet from the heat and place the fish pieces in the paste without breaking up the fish. Return the skillet to the heat, add the water, and cook over medium heat for 15–20 minutes. Transfer to a warmed serving dish, garnish with chopped cilantro, and serve with Indian bread.

Fish in Coconut

Fish and seafood play an important role in Thai cuisine, with many regions having their own specialties. If you like seafood, you will love this appetizing dish, which combines delicate whitefish with tender squid and juicy shrimp.

SERVES 4

2 tbsp vegetable oil or peanut oil

6 scallions, roughly chopped

1-inch/2.5-cm piece fresh ginger, grated

2–3 tbsp Thai red curry paste

1¾ cups coconut milk

⅔ cup fish stock

4 kaffir lime leaves

1 lemongrass stalk, broken in half

12 oz/350 g whitefish fillets, skinned and
   cut into chunks

8 oz/225 g squid rings and tentacles

8 oz/225 g large cooked peeled shrimp

1 tbsp fish sauce

2 tbsp Thai soy sauce

4 tbsp snipped fresh Chinese chives

cooked jasmine rice with chopped fresh
   cilantro, to serve

Heat the oil in a wok or large skillet and stir-fry the scallions and ginger for 1–2 minutes. Add the curry paste and stir-fry for 1–2 minutes.

Add the coconut milk, fish stock, lime leaves, and lemongrass. Bring to a boil, then reduce the heat and let simmer for 1 minute.

Add the fish, squid, and shrimp, and let simmer for 2–3 minutes, until the fish is cooked. Add the fish sauce and soy sauce and stir in the chives. Serve immediately, accompanied by cooked jasmine rice with chopped cilantro stirred through it.

Goan-Style Seafood Curry

With mustard seeds, curry leaves, and a creamy coconut sauce, this quick and easy dish could have originated anywhere in southern India, not just in tropical Goa on the west coast. Coconut is a very common ingredient in Goan cooking and both the flesh and milk are used in sweet and savory dishes.

SERVES 4-6

3 tbsp vegetable oil or peanut oil

1 tbsp black mustard seeds

12 fresh or 1 tbsp dried curry leaves

6 shallots, finely chopped

1 garlic clove, crushed

1 tsp ground turmeric

½ tsp ground coriander

¼–½ tsp chili powder

scant 3 cups coconut cream

1 lb 2 oz/500 g whitefish fillets, cut into large chunks

1 lb/450 g large raw shrimp, peeled and deveined

juice and finely grated rind of 1 lime

salt

Heat the oil in a wok or large skillet over high heat. Add the mustard seeds and stir them around for about 1 minute, or until they pop. Stir in the curry leaves.

Add the shallots and garlic and stir for about 5 minutes, or until the shallots are golden. Stir in the turmeric, coriander, and chili powder and continue stirring for about 30 seconds.

Add the coconut cream. Bring to a boil, then reduce the heat to medium and stir for about 2 minutes.

Reduce the heat to low, add the fish, and simmer for 1 minute, spooning the sauce over the fish and very gently spooning it around. Add the shrimp and continue to simmer for an additional 4–5 minutes, until the fish flakes easily and the shrimp turn pink and curl.

Add half the lime juice, then taste and add more lime juice and salt to taste. Sprinkle with the lime rind and serve.

Mixed Seafood Curry

This curry is a seafood-lover's dream, combining beneficial oil-rich fish with succulent shrimp, tender squid, and mouthwatering mussels in an aromatic coconut sauce. Serve with lime wedges for squeezing over.

SERVES 4

1 tbsp vegetable oil or peanut oil

3 shallots, finely chopped

1-inch/2.5-cm piece fresh galangal, peeled and thinly sliced

2 garlic cloves, finely chopped

1¾ cups coconut milk

2 lemongrass stalks, broken in half

4 tbsp fish sauce

2 tbsp chili sauce

8 oz/225 g raw jumbo shrimp, peeled and deveined

8 oz/225 g baby squid, cleaned and thickly sliced

8 oz/225 g salmon fillet, skinned and cut into chunks

6 oz/175 g tuna steak, cut into chunks

8 oz/225 g live mussels, scrubbed and debearded

lime wedges, to garnish

cooked rice, to serve

Heat the oil in a large wok with a tight-fitting lid and stir-fry the shallots, galangal, and garlic for 1–2 minutes, until they start to soften. Add the coconut milk, lemongrass, fish sauce, and chili sauce. Bring to a boil, reduce the heat, and let simmer for 1–2 minutes.

Add the shrimp, squid, salmon, and tuna, and let simmer for 3–4 minutes, until the shrimp have turned pink and the fish is cooked.

Discard any mussels with broken shells or any that refuse to close when tapped with a knife. Add the remaining mussels to the wok and cover with a lid. Let simmer for 1–2 minutes, until they have opened. Discard any mussels that remain closed. Garnish with lime wedges and serve immediately with cooked rice.

Fish in Tomato & Chili Sauce with Fried Onion

This delicious dish, in which firm-fleshed fish is shallow-fried until browned, then simmered in an alluringly spiced chili and tomato sauce, is from unexplored northeastern India. This is best served with plain boiled rice.

SERVES 4

1 lb 9 oz/700 g tilapia fillets, cut into
   2-inch/5-cm pieces

2 tbsp lemon juice

1 tsp salt, or to taste

1 tsp ground turmeric

4 tbsp sunflower oil or olive oil, plus
   extra for shallow-frying

2 tsp sugar

1 large onion, finely chopped

2 tsp ginger paste

2 tsp garlic paste

½ tsp ground fennel seeds

1 tsp ground coriander

½–1 tsp chili powder

6 oz/175 g canned chopped tomatoes

1¼ cups warm water

2–3 tbsp chopped fresh cilantro leaves

cooked basmati rice, to serve

Lay the fish on a large plate and gently rub in the lemon juice, ½ teaspoon of the salt, and ½ teaspoon of the turmeric. Set aside for 15–20 minutes.

Pour enough oil to cover the bottom of a 9-inch/23-cm skillet to a depth of about ½ inch/1 cm and place over medium–high heat. When the oil is hot, fry the pieces of fish, in a single layer, until well browned on both sides and a light crust is formed. Drain on paper towels.

Heat the 4 tablespoons of oil in a medium saucepan or skillet over medium heat and add the sugar. Let it brown, watching it carefully because once it browns it will blacken quickly. As soon as the sugar is brown, add the onion and cook for 5 minutes, until softened. Add the ginger and garlic pastes and cook for an additional 3–4 minutes, or until the mixture begins to brown.

Add the ground fennel, coriander, chili powder, and the remaining turmeric. Cook for about 1 minute, then add half the tomatoes. Stir and cook until the tomato juice has evaporated, then add the remaining tomatoes. Continue to cook, stirring, until the oil separates from the spice paste.

Pour in the warm water and add the remaining salt. Bring to a boil and reduce the heat to medium. Add the fish, stir gently, and reduce the heat to low. Cook, uncovered, for 5–6 minutes, then stir in half the cilantro leaves, and remove from the heat. Serve garnished with the remaining chopped cilantro and accompanied by cooked basmati rice.

Fish Korma

Contrary to general belief, korma is not a dish but one of the techniques used in Indian cooking. Fish korma is easy to cook and has an inviting appearance as well as an irresistible aroma and taste.

SERVES 4

1 lb 9 oz/700 g tilapia fillets, cut into
  2-inch/5-cm pieces

1 tbsp lemon juice

1 tsp salt

½ cup raw unsalted cashews

3 tbsp sunflower oil or olive oil

2-inch/5-cm piece cinnamon stick,
  halved

4 green cardamom pods, bruised

2 cloves

1 large onion, finely chopped

1–2 fresh green chiles, chopped
  (seeded if you like)

2 tsp ginger paste

2 tsp garlic paste

⅔ cup light cream

¼ cup plain yogurt

¼ tsp ground turmeric

½ tsp sugar

1 tbsp toasted slivered almonds,
  to garnish

Indian bread or cooked basmati rice,
  to serve

Place the fish on a large plate and gently rub in the lemon juice and ½ teaspoon of the salt. Set aside for 20 minutes. Soak the cashews in boiling water for 15 minutes.

Heat the oil in a wide shallow saucepan over low heat and add the cinnamon, cardamom, and cloves. Let them sizzle for 30–40 seconds.

Add the onion, chiles, ginger paste, and garlic paste. Increase the heat slightly and cook, stirring frequently, for 9–10 minutes, until the onion is very soft.

Meanwhile, drain the cashews and process them with the cream and yogurt.

Stir the turmeric into the onion mixture and add the processed ingredients, the remaining salt, and the sugar. Mix thoroughly and arrange the fish in the sauce in a single layer. Bring to a slow simmer, cover the pan, and cook for 5 minutes. Remove the lid and shake the pan gently from side to side. Spoon some of the sauce over the pieces of fish. Re-cover and cook for an additional 3–4 minutes. Transfer to a serving dish and garnish with the slivered almonds. Serve with Indian bread or cooked basmati rice.

Fish in Spicy Coconut Broth

Known as moh hin gha, *this is Burma's national dish, without which no festival is complete. Hawkers carry all the ingredients and a container of charcoal fire across a bamboo pole to cook it during festivals and fairs. Moh hin gha is served with an assortment of accompaniments, such as rice noodles, fish cakes, fried chiles, chopped onions, and any kind of fritters. It is an ideal dinner party dish.*

SERVES 6

1 lb/450 g tilapia fillets

3 cups hot water

1 lemongrass stalk

2-inch/5-cm piece fresh ginger

5–6 shallots or 1 large onion, coarsely
    chopped

2 fresh red chiles, coarsely chopped
    (seeded if you like)

4 large garlic cloves, coarsely chopped

4 tbsp peanut oil

1 tsp ground turmeric

1 tsp shrimp paste

1 tbsp fish sauce

1 lb 2 oz/500 g canned bamboo shoots
    in water

1¾ cups coconut milk

salt

TO SERVE

7 oz/200 g rice noodles, cooked
    according to the instructions on the
    package

4 hard-cooked eggs

8 dried red chiles, fried in a little oil until
    slightly blackened

4 scallions (white part only), chopped

lime or lemon wedges (optional)

fish cakes or fritters

Put the fish in a large saucepan and pour in the hot water. Slice half the lemongrass and half the ginger and add to the fish. Coarsely chop the remaining lemongrass and ginger and set aside. Bring the pan of fish to a boil, reduce the heat to low, and simmer for 5–6 minutes. Switch off the heat, cover the pan, and let the ginger and lemongrass steep in the stock for 15–20 minutes.

Meanwhile, put the shallots, red chiles, garlic, the remaining lemongrass, and the remaining ginger in a food processor or blender and process until mushy.

Heat the oil in a large saucepan over medium heat, add the shallot mixture and turmeric, and cook, stirring frequently, for 10–12 minutes, reducing the heat for the last few minutes of cooking. Sprinkle over a little water, if necessary, to prevent the mixture from sticking.

Strain the reserved fish stock, reserving the fish, add enough water to make it up to 3 cups, then pour into the pan along with the shrimp paste and fish sauce. Simmer over low heat while you prepare the bamboo shoots. Drain the bamboo shoots and chop into bite-size pieces, then add to the pan with the coconut milk. Add salt to taste; both the shrimp paste and the fish sauce are salty so make sure to taste before adding salt.

Break up the tilapia fillets into small pieces and add to the pan. Simmer, uncovered, for 5–6 minutes.

To serve, place the noodles in a bowl and top it up with the broth. Serve all the other accompaniments separately so everyone can help themselves.

Penang Fish Curry

Malaysian fish and shellfish curries are very popular all over southeast Asia. This recipe, from Penang in western Malaysia, is a delicious combination of spices and flavorings, such as shallots, red chiles, ginger, and turmeric. A characteristic ingredient in Malaysian cooking is the candle nut, but, because these are only available in Asian stores, this recipe uses roasted peanuts instead to enrich, thicken, and add a nutty taste to the sauce.

SERVES 4

¼ cup dry-roasted peanuts

8–10 shallots or 2 onions, coarsely chopped

2–3 fresh red chiles, coarsely chopped

1-inch/2.5-cm piece fresh ginger, coarsely chopped

4 large garlic cloves, coarsely chopped

1 tsp shrimp paste

4 tbsp peanut oil

1 tsp ground turmeric

½ tsp chili powder

scant 2 cups warm water

½ tsp salt, or to taste

2 tbsp tamarind juice

½ tsp sugar

1 lb 9 oz/700 g skinless trout fillets, cut into ½-inch/1-cm slices

fresh cilantro sprigs, to garnish

cooked basmati rice, to serve

Put the peanuts, shallots, chiles, ginger, garlic, and shrimp paste in a food processor or blender and process until the mixture is mushy. Remove and set aside.

Heat the oil in a large shallow saucepan, preferably nonstick, and add the peanut mixture, turmeric, and chili powder. Cook over medium heat, stirring frequently, until the mixture begins to brown, then continue to cook until the mixture is fragrant, occasionally adding a little water to prevent the mixture from sticking to the bottom of the pan. This process will take 10–12 minutes.

Pour in the warm water and add the salt, tamarind juice, and sugar. Stir and mix well and carefully add the fish. Stir gently to make sure that the fish is covered with the sauce. Cover the pan, reduce the heat to low, and cook for 8–10 minutes. Remove from the heat and serve garnished with cilantro sprigs and accompanied by cooked basmati rice.

Tandoori Shrimp

Quick and easy, this is one of the ways large jumbo shrimp are cooked in ramshackle-looking beach shacks along the Goan coast. Locals and tourists alike stroll along the sandy beaches and stop for just-cooked fish and shellfish served the way it always should be: ultra-fresh and simply cooked.

SERVES 4

4 tbsp plain yogurt

2 fresh green chiles, seeded and
  chopped

½ tbsp garlic and ginger paste

seeds from 4 green cardamom pods

2 tsp ground cumin

1 tsp tomato paste

¼ tsp ground turmeric

¼ tsp salt

pinch of chili powder, ideally Kashmiri
  chili powder

24 raw jumbo shrimp, thawed if frozen,
  peeled, deveined, and tails left intact

oil, for greasing

lemon or lime wedges, to serve

Put the yogurt, chiles, and garlic and ginger paste in a small food processor or spice grinder and process to a paste. Alternatively use a pestle and mortar. Transfer the paste to a large nonmetallic bowl and stir in the cardamom seeds, cumin, tomato paste, turmeric, salt, and chili powder.

Add the shrimp to the bowl and use your hands to make sure they are coated with the yogurt marinade. Cover the bowl with plastic wrap and chill for at least 30 minutes, or up to 4 hours.

When you are ready to cook, heat a large grill pan or skillet over high heat until a few drops of water "dance" when they hit the surface. Use crumpled paper towels or a pastry brush to grease the hot pan very lightly with oil.

Use tongs to lift the shrimp out of the marinade, letting the excess drip back into the bowl, then place the shrimp on the pan and cook for 2 minutes. Flip the shrimp over and cook for an additional 1–2 minutes, until they turn pink, curl, and are opaque all the way through when you cut one. Serve the shrimp immediately with lemon or lime wedges for squeezing over.

COOK'S TIP

The spiced yogurt mixture also makes an excellent marinade for tandoori seafood kabobs. Cut 1 lb 10 oz/750 g thick whitefish fillets, such as cod or monkfish, into 1½-inch/4-cm cubes and put in the marinade with 12 or 16 large shelled and deveined shrimp. Let marinate for at least 30 minutes, or up to 4 hours. Thread the fish and shrimp onto six greased metal skewers, alternating with pieces of blanched red or green bell peppers and/or white mushrooms. Cook under a preheated broiler for about 15 minutes, turning the skewers and brushing with any leftover marinade frequently, until the fish flakes easily and the edges are lightly charred.

Shrimp Biryani

This tantalizing dish is packed with warming, aromatic spices and tinged golden with saffron. Biryani dishes can be time-consuming to prepare, but this cheat's version is perfect for supper in a hurry.

SERVES 8

1 tsp saffron strands

4 tbsp warm water

2 shallots, coarsely chopped

3 garlic cloves, crushed

1-inch/2.5-cm piece fresh ginger, chopped

2 tsp coriander seeds

½ tsp black peppercorns

2 cloves

seeds from 2 green cardamom pods

1-inch/2.5-cm piece cinnamon stick

1 tsp ground turmeric

1 fresh green chile, chopped

½ tsp salt

2 tbsp ghee

1 tsp black mustard seeds

1 lb 2 oz/500 g raw jumbo shrimp in their shells, or 14 oz/400 g raw jumbo shrimp, peeled and deveined

1¼ cups coconut milk

1¼ cups lowfat plain yogurt

cooked basmati rice, to serve

toasted slivered almonds and sliced scallions, to garnish

Soak the saffron in the warm water for 10 minutes. Put the shallots, garlic, ginger, coriander seeds, peppercorns, cloves, cardamom seeds, cinnamon stick, turmeric, chile, and salt into a spice grinder or mortar and grind to a paste.

Melt the ghee in a saucepan and add the mustard seeds. When they start to pop, add the shrimp and stir over high heat for 1 minute. Stir in the spice mix, then the coconut milk and yogurt. Simmer for 20 minutes.

Spoon the shrimp mixture into warmed serving dishes. Top with the cooked basmati rice and drizzle over the saffron water. Serve garnished with the slivered almonds and scallions.

Shrimp Pooris

This restaurant favorite is easy to re-create at home. The deep-fried pooris aren't difficult to make (see page 194 for the recipe), but remember to leave enough time for the dough to rest for 20 minutes before it is cooked. Serve this as an appetizer or main course, or make mini pooris and serve the shrimp mixture as a dip.

SERVES 6

2 tsp coriander seeds

½ tsp black peppercorns

1 large garlic clove, crushed

1 tsp ground turmeric

¼–½ tsp chili powder

½ tsp salt

3 tbsp ghee, vegetable oil, or peanut oil

1 onion, grated

1 lb 12 oz/800 g canned crushed tomatoes

pinch of sugar

1 lb 2 oz/500 g small cooked peeled shrimp, thawed if frozen

½ tsp garam masala, plus extra to garnish

6 Pooris, kept warm (see page 194)

chopped fresh cilantro, to garnish

Put the coriander seeds, peppercorns, garlic, turmeric, chili powder, and salt in a small food processor, spice grinder, or mortar and blend to a thick paste.

Melt the ghee in a wok or large skillet over medium–low heat. Add the paste and cook, stirring continuously, for about 30 seconds.

Add the grated onion and stir for an additional 30 seconds. Stir in the tomatoes and the sugar. Bring to a boil, stirring, and let bubble for 10 minutes, mashing the tomatoes against the side of the wok to break them down, or until reduced. Taste and add extra salt, if necessary.

Add the shrimp and sprinkle with the garam masala. When the shrimp are hot, arrange the hot pooris on plates and top each one with a portion of the shrimp. Sprinkle with the cilantro and garam masala and serve.

COOK'S TIP

Deep-fried pooris are best served straight from the wok, so it is a good idea to have a couple of woks to use if you are entertaining. The pooris, with their rich, light texture, are traditional with this dish, but chapattis or naans are also good, especially if you want to avoid last-minute deep-frying.

Shrimp in Coconut Milk with Chiles & Curry Leaves

This chile-spiked, turmeric-tinged shrimp curry is mellowed with coconut milk and distinctively flavored with curry leaves, which are available fresh in Asian stores and dried in large supermarkets. Fresh ones can be frozen for up to three months.

SERVES 4

4 tbsp sunflower oil or olive oil

½ tsp black or brown mustard seeds

½ tsp fenugreek seeds

1 large onion, finely chopped

2 tsp garlic paste

2 tsp ginger paste

1–2 fresh green chiles, chopped (seeded if you like)

1 tbsp ground coriander

½ tsp ground turmeric

½ tsp chili powder

1 tsp salt, or to taste

generous 1 cup coconut milk

1 lb/450 g cooked peeled jumbo shrimp, thawed and drained if frozen

1 tbsp tamarind juice or juice of ½ lime

½ tsp crushed black peppercorns

10–12 fresh or dried curry leaves

Heat 3 tablespoons of the oil in a medium saucepan over medium–high heat. When hot, but not smoking, add the mustard seeds, followed by the fenugreek seeds and the onion. Cook, stirring frequently, for 5–6 minutes, until the onion is softened but not browned. Add the garlic and ginger pastes and the chiles and cook, stirring frequently, for an additional 5–6 minutes, until the onion is a light golden color.

Add the coriander, turmeric, and chili powder and cook, stirring, for 1 minute. Add the salt and coconut milk, followed by the shrimp and tamarind juice. Bring to a slow simmer and cook, stirring occasionally, for 3–4 minutes.

Meanwhile, heat the remaining oil in a very small saucepan over medium heat. Add the peppercorns and curry leaves. Turn off the heat and let sizzle for 20–25 seconds, then fold the aromatic oil into the shrimp mixture. Remove from the heat and serve immediately.

Chili Shrimp with Garlic Noodles

A hot and spicy dish for those chile enthusiasts! The crunchy snow peas and bean sprouts complement the hot flavors well.

SERVES 4

7 oz/200 g cooked peeled jumbo shrimp

4 tbsp sweet chili sauce

4 tbsp peanut oil or vegetable oil

4 scallions, chopped

2 oz/55 g snow peas, trimmed and
   halved diagonally

1 tbsp Thai red curry paste

1¾ cups coconut milk

2 oz/55 g canned bamboo shoots,
   drained

⅓ cup fresh bean sprouts

GARLIC NOODLES

4 oz/115 g dried medium egg noodles

2 garlic cloves, crushed

handful of fresh cilantro, chopped

salt

Toss the shrimp with the chili sauce in a bowl. Cover and set aside.

Heat half the oil in a preheated wok. Add the scallions and snow peas, then stir-fry over medium–high heat for 2–3 minutes. Add the curry paste and stir well. Pour in the coconut milk and bring gently to a boil, stirring occasionally. Add the bamboo shoots and bean sprouts and cook, stirring, for 1 minute. Stir in the shrimp and chili sauce, then reduce the heat and simmer for 1–2 minutes, or until just heated through.

Meanwhile, bring a saucepan of lightly salted water to a boil, add the noodles, and cook for 4–5 minutes, until just tender, or according to the package directions. Drain and return to the pan.

Heat the remaining oil in a small nonstick skillet, then add the garlic and stir-fry over high heat for 30 seconds. Add to the drained noodles with half the cilantro and toss together until well mixed.

Transfer the garlic noodles to serving bowls. Top with the shrimp mixture and serve immediately, garnished with the remaining cilantro.

Shrimp with Scallions & Straw Mushrooms

Straw mushrooms are widely used in Asian cooking and take their name from the paddy straw on which they are grown. Canned straw mushrooms are available from Asian stores.

SERVES 4

2 tbsp vegetable oil or peanut oil

1 bunch of scallions, chopped

2 garlic cloves, finely chopped

1¼ cups coconut cream

2 tbsp Thai red curry paste

1 cup fish stock

2 tbsp fish sauce

2 tbsp Thai soy sauce

6 fresh Thai basil sprigs

14 oz/400 g canned straw mushrooms, drained

12 oz/350 g large cooked peeled shrimp

cooked jasmine rice, to serve

Heat the oil in a wok and stir-fry the scallions and garlic for 2–3 minutes. Add the coconut cream, curry paste, and stock and bring just to a boil.

Stir in the fish sauce and soy sauce, then add the basil, mushrooms, and shrimp. Gradually bring to a boil and serve immediately with cooked jasmine rice.

Goan Shrimp Curry with Hard-Cooked Eggs

Goa, on the west coast of India, has a cuisine rich in culture and religion. The influence of not only the indigenous Hindu faith, but also Islam and Christianity, both of which came with foreign invaders, has placed Goan cuisine in a unique position. In this recipe, large shrimp and hard-cooked eggs are bathed in rich, aromatic coconut milk.

SERVES 4

4 tbsp sunflower oil or olive oil

1 large onion, finely chopped

2 tsp ginger paste

2 tsp garlic paste

2 tsp ground coriander

½ tsp ground fennel

½ tsp ground turmeric

½–1 tsp chili powder

½ tsp pepper

2–3 tbsp water

4½ oz/125 g canned chopped tomatoes

scant 1 cup coconut milk

1 tsp salt, or to taste

4 hard-cooked eggs

1 lb 9 oz/700 g cooked peeled jumbo
  shrimp

juice of 1 lime

2–3 tbsp chopped fresh cilantro leaves

cooked basmati rice, to serve

Heat the oil in a medium saucepan over medium–high heat and add the onion. Cook until the onion is softened but not browned. Add the ginger paste and garlic paste and cook for 2–3 minutes.

In a small bowl, combine the coriander, ground fennel, turmeric, chili powder, and pepper. Add the water and make a paste. Reduce the heat to medium, add the paste to the onion mixture, and cook for 1–2 minutes. Reduce the heat to low and continue to cook for 3–4 minutes.

Add half the tomatoes and cook for 2–3 minutes. Add the remaining tomatoes and cook for an additional 2–3 minutes.

Add the coconut milk and salt, bring to a slow simmer, and cook, uncovered, for 6–8 minutes, stirring frequently.

Meanwhile, shell the eggs and, using a sharp knife, make 4 slits lengthwise on each egg without cutting through. Add the eggs to the pan along with the shrimp. Increase the heat slightly and cook for 6–8 minutes.

Stir in the lime juice and half the cilantro. Remove from the heat and transfer the curry to a serving dish. Garnish with the remaining cilantro and serve with cooked basmati rice.

Mussels with Mustard Seeds & Shallots

Baskets piled high with fresh mussels are not an uncommon slight along India's southern Malabar coast. Quickly cooked, fragrant dishes colored with golden turmeric such as this are served in the open-air restaurants along Kochi's harborside, alongside the picturesque fishing nets.

SERVES 4

4 lb 8 oz/2 kg live mussels, scrubbed and debearded

3 tbsp vegetable oil or peanut oil

½ tbsp black mustard seeds

8 shallots, chopped

2 garlic cloves, crushed

2 tbsp distilled vinegar

4 small fresh red chiles

1¼ cups coconut cream

10 fresh or 1 tbsp dried curry leaves

½ tsp ground turmeric

¼–½ tsp chili powder

salt

Discard any mussels with broken shells or any that refuse to close when tapped with a knife. Set aside.

Heat the oil in a wok or large skillet over medium–high heat. Add the mustard seeds and stir them around for 1 minute, or until they start to pop.

Add the shallots and garlic and cook, stirring frequently, for 3 minutes, or until they start to brown. Stir in the vinegar, whole chiles, coconut cream, curry leaves, turmeric, chili powder, and a pinch of salt and bring to a boil, stirring.

Reduce the heat to very low. Add the mussels, cover the wok, and let the mussels simmer, shaking the wok frequently, for 3–4 minutes, or until they are all open. Discard any mussels that remain closed. Ladle the mussels into deep bowls, then taste the broth and add extra salt, if necessary. Spoon over the mussels and serve.

COOK'S TIP

Taste the bright yellow broth before you add it to the mussels. If the mussels are gritty, strain the liquid through a strainer lined with cheesecloth or paper towels. Mussels should be cooked on the day of purchase.

Vegetables & Pulses

Vegetable Korma

The korma style of cooking was originally used only for meat and poultry. However, its popularity is so overwhelming that various vegetarian recipes have been created in recent years. The dish is a subtle sensation of flavors and a total visual delight.

SERVES 4

½ cup raw cashews

¾ cup boiling water

good pinch of saffron threads, pounded

2 tbsp hot milk

1 small head cauliflower, divided into
  ½-inch/1-cm florets

4 oz/115 g green beans, cut into
  1-inch/2.5-cm lengths

4 oz/115 g carrots, cut into
  1-inch/2.5-cm sticks

9 oz/250 g young, waxy potatoes, boiled
  in their skins and cooled

4 tbsp sunflower oil or olive oil

1 large onion, finely chopped

2 tsp ginger paste

1–2 fresh green chiles, chopped
  (seeded if you like)

2 tsp ground coriander

½ tsp ground turmeric

6 tbsp warm water

1¾ cups good-quality vegetable stock

½ tsp salt, or to taste

2 tbsp light cream

2 tsp ghee or butter

1 tsp garam masala

½ tsp grated nutmeg

Soak the cashews in the boiling water in a heatproof bowl for 20 minutes. Meanwhile, soak the pounded saffron in the hot milk. Blanch the vegetables, one at a time, in a saucepan of boiling water: blanch the cauliflower for 3 minutes, drain, and immediately plunge in cold water; blanch the green beans for 3 minutes, drain, and plunge in cold water; and blanch the carrots for 4 minutes, drain, and plunge in cold water. Peel the potatoes, if you like, and halve or quarter them according to their size.

Heat the oil in a medium heavy-bottom saucepan over medium heat. Add the onion, ginger paste, and chiles and cook, stirring frequently, for 5–6 minutes, until the onion is softened. Add the coriander and turmeric and cook, stirring, for 1 minute. Add 3 tablespoons of the warm water and cook for 2–3 minutes. Add the remaining warm water, then cook, stirring frequently, for 2–3 minutes, or until the oil separates from the spice paste.

Add the stock, saffron and milk mixture, and salt, and bring to a boil. Drain the vegetables, add to the saucepan, and return to a boil. Reduce the heat to low and simmer for 2–3 minutes.

Meanwhile, put the cashews and their soaking water in a food processor and process until well blended. Add to the korma, then stir in the cream. Let stand over very low heat while you prepare the final seasoning. Melt the ghee in a very small saucepan over low heat. Add the garam masala and nutmeg and let the spices sizzle gently for 20–25 seconds. Fold the spiced butter into the korma. Remove from the heat and serve immediately.

COOK'S TIP

You can store this korma in the refrigerator for 3–4 days, but reheat very gently, adding a little warm water to maintain the consistency of the sauce.

Vietnamese Vegetable Curry

Curries are popular in South Vietnam, where Indian-influenced spicy foods are enjoyed. This vegetable and tofu curry can be served with French baguette (the classic way), rice, or noodles.

SERVES 6

2 lemongrass stalks

¼ cup vegetable oil

3 large garlic cloves, crushed

1 large shallot, thinly sliced

2 tbsp Indian curry powder

3 cups coconut milk

2 cups coconut water (not coconut milk) or vegetable stock

2 tbsp fish sauce

4 fresh red Thai chiles or dried red Chinese (tien sien) chiles

6 kaffir lime leaves

1 carrot, peeled and cut diagonally into ½ inch/1 cm thick pieces

1 small–medium Asian eggplant, cut into 1-inch/2.5-cm pieces

1 small–medium bamboo shoot, cut into thin wedges

1 cup snow peas, trimmed

12 large shiitake mushrooms, stems discarded, caps halved

1 lb/450 g firm or extra-firm tofu, drained and cut into 1-inch/2.5-cm cubes

fresh Thai basil leaves and fried shallots, to garnish

Discard the bruised leaves and root ends of the lemongrass stalks, then cut 6–8 inches/15–20 cm of the lower stalks into paper-thin slices.

Heat the oil in a large saucepan over high heat, add the garlic and shallot, and stir-fry for 5 minutes, or until golden. Add the lemongrass and curry powder and stir-fry for 2 minutes, or until fragrant. Add the coconut milk, coconut water, fish sauce, chiles, and lime leaves and bring to a boil. Reduce the heat to low, then add the carrot and eggplant, cover, and cook for 10 minutes.

Add the bamboo shoot, snow peas, mushrooms, and tofu and cook for an additional 5 minutes.

Serve, garnished with the basil leaves and fried shallots.

COOK'S TIP

Boiled and vacuum-packed whole bamboo shoots from Japan are the best. These can be sliced and used without any additional preparation. If using fresh bamboo, be sure to peel and boil the shoot for 10 minutes in water before using in the recipe. If using frozen raw bamboo, do the same. If using canned bamboo, be sure to use a whole shoot rather than precut shoots. Bamboo shoots have the ability to absorb flavor. For this reason, canned bamboo must be boiled for 2 minutes to eliminate any flavor from the can.

Carrot & Pumpkin Curry

This creamy carrot and pumpkin curry, with its gorgeous fall colors, is perfect comfort food. It is equally delicious made with butternut squash instead of the pumpkin.

SERVES 4

⅔ cup vegetable stock

1-inch piece fresh galangal, sliced

2 garlic cloves, chopped

1 lemongrass stalk (white part only),
    finely chopped

2 fresh red chiles, seeded and chopped

4 carrots, peeled and cut into chunks

8 oz/225 g pumpkin, peeled, seeded,
    and cut into cubes

2 tbsp vegetable oil or peanut oil

2 shallots, finely chopped

3 tbsp Thai yellow curry paste

1¾ cups coconut milk

4–6 fresh Thai basil sprigs

⅛ cup toasted pumpkin seeds,
    to garnish

Pour the stock into a large saucepan and bring to a boil. Add the galangal, half the garlic, the lemongrass, and chiles, and let simmer for 5 minutes. Add the carrots and pumpkin and let simmer for 5–6 minutes, until tender.

Meanwhile, heat the oil in a wok or skillet and stir-fry the shallots and the remaining garlic for 2–3 minutes. Add the curry paste and stir-fry for 1–2 minutes.

Stir the shallot mixture into the pan and add the coconut milk and Thai basil. Let simmer for 2–3 minutes. Serve hot, sprinkled with the toasted pumpkin seeds.

Vegetables with Tofu & Spinach

Tofu has been a staple protein in much of Asia for many centuries and is renowned for its ability to absorb whatever flavoring it is mixed with. Here it is deep-fried until crisp and used as a topping for a creamy Thai-style vegetable curry.

SERVES 4

vegetable oil or peanut oil,
   for deep-frying
8 oz/225 g firm tofu, drained and cut
   into cubes
2 tbsp vegetable oil or peanut oil
2 onions, chopped
2 garlic cloves, chopped
1 fresh red chile, seeded and sliced
3 celery stalks, diagonally sliced
8 oz/225 g mushrooms, thickly sliced
4 oz/115 g baby corn, halved
1 red bell pepper, seeded and cut into
   strips
3 tbsp Thai red curry paste
1¾ cups coconut milk
1 tsp jaggery or light brown sugar
2 tbsp Thai soy sauce
5 cups baby spinach leaves

Heat the oil for deep-frying in a skillet and deep-fry the tofu cubes, in batches, for 4–5 minutes, until crisp and browned. Remove with a slotted spoon and drain on paper towels.

Heat the 2 tablespoons of oil in a skillet and stir-fry the onions, garlic, and chile for 1–2 minutes, until they start to soften. Add the celery, mushrooms, corn, and red bell pepper, and stir-fry for 3–4 minutes, until they soften.

Stir in the curry paste and coconut milk and gradually bring to a boil. Add the jaggery and soy sauce and then the spinach. Cook, stirring continuously, until the spinach has wilted. Serve immediately, topped with the tofu.

Red Curry with Mixed Leaves

This eye-catching mixture of green shoots and leaves should be cooked quickly to retain the varied textures of the ingredients.

SERVES 4

2 tbsp peanut oil or vegetable oil

2 onions, thinly sliced

1 bunch of fine asparagus spears

1¾ cups coconut milk

2 tbsp Thai red curry paste

3 fresh kaffir lime leaves

8 oz/225 g baby spinach leaves

2 heads bok choy, chopped

1 small head Chinese cabbage, shredded

handful of fresh cilantro, chopped

cooked rice, to serve

Heat the oil in a preheated wok. Add the onions and asparagus and stir-fry over medium–high heat for 1–2 minutes.

Add the coconut milk, curry paste, and lime leaves and bring gently to a boil, stirring occasionally. Add the spinach, bok choy, and Chinese cabbage and cook, stirring, for 2–3 minutes, or until wilted. Add the cilantro and stir well. Serve immediately with rice.

COOK'S TIP

For nonvegetarians, sprinkle some shredded or diced cooked chicken or cooked peeled shrimp over the cooked rice to accompany the curry.

Cauliflower, Eggplant & Green Bean Korma

Mild and fragrant, this slow-braised mixed vegetable dish reflects the skilled flavoring of Mogul cooking. The rich, almost velvety, cream-based sauce is spiced but doesn't contain chiles, making it an indulgent treat for anyone who prefers mild dishes.

SERVES 4–6

generous ½ cup cashews

1½ tbsp garlic and ginger paste

scant 1 cup water

4 tbsp ghee, vegetable oil, or peanut oil

1 large onion, chopped

5 green cardamom pods, bruised

1 cinnamon stick, broken in half

¼ tsp ground turmeric

generous 1 cup heavy cream

5 oz/140 g new potatoes, scrubbed and chopped into ½-inch/1-cm pieces

140 g/5 oz cauliflower florets

½ tsp garam masala

5 oz/140 g eggplant, chopped into 1-inch/2.5-cm chunks

5 oz/140 g green beans, chopped into 1-inch/2.5-cm lengths

salt and pepper

chopped fresh mint or cilantro, to garnish

Heat a large flameproof casserole or skillet with a tight-fitting lid over high heat. Add the cashews and stir them until they start to brown, then immediately turn them out of the casserole.

Put the nuts in a spice grinder with the garlic and ginger paste and 1 tablespoon of the water and process to a coarse paste.

Melt half the ghee in the casserole over medium–high heat. Add the onion and sauté for 5–8 minutes, until golden brown.

Add the nut paste and stir for 5 minutes. Stir in the cardamom pods, cinnamon stick, and turmeric.

Add the cream and the remaining water and bring to a boil, stirring. Reduce the heat to the lowest level, cover the casserole, and simmer for 5 minutes.

Add the potatoes, cauliflower, and garam masala and simmer, covered, for 5 minutes. Stir in the eggplant and green beans and continue simmering for an additional 5 minutes, or until all the vegetables are tender. Check the sauce occasionally to make sure it isn't sticking on the bottom of the pan, and stir in a little water if needed.

Taste and add seasoning, if necessary. Sprinkle with the mint or cilantro and serve.

Broccoli with Peanuts

This innovative dish combines fragrant spices with tender vegetables and is perfect for making broccoli more appealing. The tasty topping of crunchy peanuts adds texture and interest.

SERVES 4

3 tbsp vegetable oil or peanut oil

1 lemongrass stalk, coarsely chopped

2 fresh red chiles, seeded and chopped

1-inch/2.5-cm piece fresh ginger, grated

3 kaffir lime leaves, coarsely torn

3 tbsp Thai green curry paste

1 onion, chopped

1 red bell pepper, seeded and chopped

12 oz/350 g head broccoli, cut into
   florets

4 oz/115 g fine green beans

scant ½ cup unsalted peanuts

Put 2 tablespoons of the oil, the lemongrass, chiles, ginger, lime leaves, and curry paste into a food processor or blender and process to a paste.

Heat the remaining oil in a wok, add the spice paste, onion, and bell pepper, and stir-fry for 2–3 minutes, until the vegetables start to soften.

Add the broccoli and green beans, cover, and cook over low heat, stirring occasionally, for 4–5 minutes, until tender.

Meanwhile, toast or dry-fry the peanuts until lightly browned. Add them to the broccoli mixture and toss together. Serve immediately.

Okra Stir-Fried with Onions

Okra stir-fried with onions and spices makes a superb side dish. Here, the combination of the soft green okra, bright red bell pepper, and white onion, all dotted with black mustard seeds, creates a colorful, appetizing effect.

SERVES 4

10 oz/280 g okra

1 small red bell pepper

1 onion

2 tbsp sunflower oil or olive oil

1 tsp black or brown mustard seeds

½ tsp cumin seeds

3 large garlic cloves, lightly crushed, then chopped

½ tsp chili powder

½ tsp salt, or to taste

½ tsp garam masala

cooked basmati rice, to serve

Scrub each okra gently, rinse well in cold running water, then slice off the hard head. Halve diagonally and set aside.

Seed and core the red bell pepper and cut into 1½-inch/4-cm strips. Halve the onion lengthwise and cut into ¼ inch/5 mm thick slices.

Heat the oil in a heavy-bottom skillet or wok over medium heat. When hot, but not smoking, add the mustard seeds, followed by the cumin seeds. Remove from the heat and add the garlic. Return to low heat and cook the garlic gently, stirring, for 1 minute, or until lightly browned.

Add the okra, red bell pepper, and onion, increase the heat to medium–high, and stir-fry for 2 minutes. Add the chili powder and salt and stir-fry for an additional 3 minutes. Add the garam masala and stir-fry for 1 minute. Remove from the heat and serve immediately with cooked basmati rice.

COOK'S TIP

Make sure that the oil is at the right temperature or else the mustard seeds will not release their delightful nutty taste. To test the temperature, drop 1 or 2 mustard seeds into the hot oil—if they pop straight away, the oil is just right.

Vegetables in a Creamy Tomato Sauce

There is nothing better to accompany an Asian meal than a selection of fresh vegetables in a lightly spiced sauce. The choice of the combination of vegetables can be completely flexible, but remember to choose them with visual appeal in mind. Here, carrots, potatoes, and green beans are used to create a colorful appearance.

SERVES 4

7 oz/200 g green beans, cut into
    2-inch/5-cm lengths

7 oz/200 g head cauliflower, divided into
    ½-inch/1-cm florets

7 oz/200 g baby carrots, peeled and left
    whole

7 oz/200 g boiled potatoes

4 tbsp sunflower oil or olive oil

5 green cardamom pods, bruised

2 bay leaves

1 large onion, finely chopped

1-inch/2.5-cm piece fresh ginger, finely
    grated

1 tsp ground coriander

½ tsp ground cumin

1 tsp ground turmeric

½–1 tsp chili powder

1 tbsp tomato paste

1 tsp salt, or to taste

⅔ cup warm water

⅔ cup heavy cream

2 tomatoes, seeded and coarsely
    chopped

Indian bread or cooked basmati rice,
    to serve

Blanch all the raw vegetables separately (the green beans will need 3 minutes, the cauliflower 3 minutes, and the carrots 5 minutes), then plunge them into cold water. Cut the potatoes into 1-inch/2.5-cm cubes.

Heat the oil in a medium saucepan over low heat and add the cardamom and bay leaves. Let them sizzle for 30–40 seconds, then add the onion and ginger. Increase the heat to medium and cook for 5–6 minutes, until the onion is softened, stirring frequently.

Add the coriander, cumin, turmeric, and chili powder. Cook for 2–3 minutes, add a little water, and continue to cook for an additional minute. Add the tomato paste and cook for about 1 minute.

Drain the green beans, cauliflower, and carrots and add to the pan along with the potatoes. Add the salt, stir, and pour in the warm water. Cook, uncovered, for 2–3 minutes, then add the cream. Cook for 3–4 minutes, fold in the tomatoes, and remove from the heat. Serve with Indian bread or cooked basmati rice.

Cumin-Scented Eggplant & Potato Curry

Chunks of eggplant, with its beautiful shiny skin, and creamy potatoes are cooked in a richly spiced tomato and onion sauce, which is aromatized with nigella seeds and intensified with fresh chiles. A delicious, healthy dish to enjoy with any Indian bread.

SERVES 4

1 large eggplant, about 12 oz/350 g

8 oz/225 g potatoes, boiled in their skins and cooled

3 tbsp sunflower oil or olive oil

½ tsp black mustard seeds

½ tsp nigella seeds

½ tsp fennel seeds

1 onion, finely chopped

1-inch/2.5-cm piece fresh ginger, grated

2 fresh green chiles, chopped (seeded if you like)

½ tsp ground cumin

1 tsp ground coriander

1 tsp ground turmeric

½ tsp chili powder

1 tbsp tomato paste

scant 2 cups warm water

1 tsp salt, or to taste

½ tsp garam masala

2 tbsp chopped fresh cilantro leaves

Indian bread, to serve

Quarter the eggplant lengthwise and cut the stem end of each quarter into 2-inch/5-cm pieces. Halve the remaining part of the quarter and cut into 2-inch/5-cm pieces. Soak the eggplant pieces in cold water.

Peel the potatoes and cut into 2-inch/5-cm cubes. Heat the oil in a large saucepan over medium heat. When hot, add the mustard seeds and, as soon as they start popping, add the nigella seeds and fennel seeds.

Add the onion, ginger, and chiles and cook for 7–8 minutes, until the mixture begins to brown.

Add the cumin, coriander, turmeric, and chili powder. Cook for about 1 minute, then add the tomato paste. Cook for an additional 1 minute, then pour in the warm water and add the salt and drained eggplant. Bring to a boil and cook over medium heat for 8–10 minutes, stirring frequently to make sure that the eggplant cooks evenly. At the start of cooking, the eggplant will float, but once it soaks up the liquid it will sink quite quickly. As soon as the eggplant sinks, add the potatoes and cook for 2–3 minutes, stirring.

Stir in the garam masala and chopped cilantro and remove from the heat. Serve with Indian bread.

Mushroom Bhaji

Mushroom bhaji is not a traditional Indian dish, but mushrooms do seem to have a certain affinity with a spiced, tomato-based sauce. It is important to choose the right combination of spices in order to complement the natural taste of the mushrooms.

SERVES 4

10 oz/280 g button mushrooms

4 tbsp sunflower oil or olive oil

1 onion, finely chopped

1 fresh green chile, finely chopped
   (seeded if you like)

2 tsp garlic paste

1 tsp ground cumin

1 tsp ground coriander

½ tsp chili powder

½ tsp salt, or to taste

1 tbsp tomato paste

3 tbsp water

1 tbsp snipped fresh chives, to garnish

Wipe the mushrooms with damp paper towels and slice thickly.

Heat the oil in a medium saucepan over medium heat. Add the onion and chile and cook, stirring, for 5–6 minutes, until the onion is softened but not browned. Add the garlic paste and cook, stirring, for 2 minutes.

Add the cumin, coriander, and chili powder and cook, stirring, for 1 minute. Add the mushrooms, salt, and tomato paste and stir until all the ingredients are blended.

Sprinkle the water evenly over the mushrooms and reduce the heat to low. Cover and cook for 10 minutes, stirring halfway through. The sauce should have thickened, but if it appears runny, cook, uncovered, for 3–4 minutes, or until you achieve the desired consistency.

Transfer to a serving dish, sprinkle the chives on top, and serve immediately.

Garden Peas & Paneer in Chili-Tomato Sauce

Paneer, or Indian cheese, is a great source of protein for the vast majority of the Indian population who don't eat meat. This is a traditional vegetarian main course where tender morsels of paneer are simmered in a spice-infused tomato sauce.

SERVES 4

4 tbsp sunflower oil or olive oil

9 oz/250 g paneer, cut into 1-inch/
   2.5-cm cubes

4 green cardamom pods, bruised

2 bay leaves

1 onion, finely chopped

2 tsp garlic paste

2 tsp ginger paste

2 tsp ground coriander

½ tsp ground turmeric

½–1 tsp chili powder

5½ oz/150 g canned chopped tomatoes

scant 2 cups warm water, plus 2 tbsp

1 tsp salt, or to taste

1¼ cups frozen peas

½ tsp garam masala

2 tbsp light cream

2 tbsp chopped fresh cilantro leaves

Indian bread, to serve

Heat 2 tablespoons of the oil in a medium nonstick saucepan over medium heat. Add the paneer and cook, stirring frequently, for 3–4 minutes, or until evenly browned. Paneer tends to splatter in hot oil, so stand slightly away from the stove. Alternatively, use a splatter screen. Remove and drain on paper towels.

Add the remaining oil to the saucepan and reduce the heat to low. Add the cardamom pods and bay leaves and let sizzle gently for 20–25 seconds. Add the onion, increase the heat to medium, and cook, stirring frequently, for 4–5 minutes, until the onion is softened. Add the garlic paste and ginger paste and cook, stirring frequently, for an additional 3–4 minutes, until the onion is a pale golden color.

Add the coriander, turmeric, and chili powder and cook, stirring, for 1 minute. Add the tomatoes and cook, stirring frequently, for 4–5 minutes. Add the 2 tablespoons of warm water and cook, stirring frequently, for 3 minutes, or until the oil separates from the spice paste.

Add the remaining warm water and the salt. Bring to a boil, then reduce the heat to low and simmer, uncovered, for 7–8 minutes.

Add the paneer and peas and simmer for 5 minutes. Stir in the garam masala, cream, and chopped cilantro and remove from the heat. Serve immediately with Indian bread.

Garlic & Chile Potatoes with Cauliflower

Known as aloo gobi, *this is a well-known dish that is popular in most Indian restaurants. There are as many different versions as there are cooks. This version is easy to make, can be part-prepared ahead of time, and is simply delicious!*

SERVES 4

12 oz/350 g young, waxy potatoes

1 small head cauliflower

2 tbsp sunflower oil or olive oil

1 tsp black or brown mustard seeds

1 tsp cumin seeds

5 large garlic cloves, lightly crushed, then chopped

1–2 fresh green chiles, finely chopped (seeded if you like)

½ tsp ground turmeric

½ tsp salt, or to taste

2 tbsp chopped fresh cilantro leaves

Indian bread, to serve

Cook the potatoes in their skins in a saucepan of boiling water for 20 minutes, or until tender. Drain, then soak in cold water for 30 minutes. Peel them, if you like, then halve or quarter according to their size—they should be a similar size to the cauliflower florets (see below).

Meanwhile, divide the cauliflower into about ½-inch/1-cm florets and blanch in a large saucepan of boiling water for 3 minutes. Drain and plunge into iced water to prevent further cooking, then drain again.

Heat the oil in a medium saucepan over medium heat. When hot, but not smoking, add the mustard seeds, then the cumin seeds.

Remove from the heat and add the garlic and chiles. Return to low heat and cook, stirring, until the garlic has a light brown tinge.

Stir in the turmeric, followed by the cauliflower and the potatoes. Add the salt, increase the heat slightly, and cook, stirring, until the vegetables are well blended with the spices and heated through.

Stir in the cilantro, remove from the heat, and serve immediately with Indian bread.

Potatoes with Spiced Spinach

This traditional and popular dish is easy to make and is a perfect accompaniment to most Indian meals. Generally, fresh spinach leaves are blanched and puréed, but you can use frozen puréed spinach, which cuts down on preparation time.

SERVES 4

12 oz/350 g young, waxy potatoes

9 oz/250 g spinach leaves, defrosted if frozen

3 tbsp sunflower oil or olive oil

1 large onion, finely sliced

1 fresh green chile, finely chopped (seeded if you like)

2 tsp garlic paste

2 tsp ginger paste

1 tsp ground coriander

½ tsp ground cumin

½ tsp chili powder

½ tsp ground turmeric

7 oz/200 g canned chopped tomatoes

½ tsp sugar

1 tsp salt, or to taste

3 tbsp light cream

Bring a large saucepan of lightly salted water to a boil, add the potatoes in their skins, and cook for 20 minutes, or until tender. Drain, then soak in cold water for 30 minutes. Peel them, if you like, then halve or quarter according to their size. Meanwhile, bring another large saucepan of lightly salted water to a boil, add the spinach and blanch for 2 minutes, then drain. Transfer to a blender or food processor and blend to a paste. Set aside.

Heat 2 tablespoons of the oil in a medium saucepan over medium heat. Add the onion and cook, stirring frequently, for 10–12 minutes, until well browned, reducing the heat to low for the last 2–3 minutes. Remove from the heat and remove the excess oil from the onion by pressing against the side of the pan with a wooden spoon. Remove and drain on paper towels.

Return the pan to the heat, add the remaining oil, and heat. Add the chile, garlic paste and ginger paste and cook over low heat, stirring, for 2–3 minutes. Add the coriander, cumin, chili powder, and turmeric and cook, stirring, for 1 minute. Add the tomatoes, increase the heat to medium, and add the sugar. Cook, stirring frequently, for 5– 6 minutes, until the tomatoes have reached a paste-like consistency.

Add the potatoes, spinach, salt, and fried onions and cook, stirring, for 2–3 minutes. Stir in the cream and cook for 1 minute. Remove from the heat and serve immediately.

Chickpeas in Coconut Milk

From the palm-fringed southern coastal area of India, where coconut milk is used as an everyday stock, this is a simple but delicious dish. Traditionally, dried chickpeas would be used, but canned chickpeas are a quick and easy alternative.

SERVES 4

10 oz/280 g potatoes, cut into
½-inch/1-cm cubes

generous 1 cup hot water

14 oz/400 g canned chickpeas, drained
and rinsed

generous 1 cup coconut milk

1 tsp salt, or to taste

2 tbsp sunflower oil or olive oil

4 large garlic cloves, finely chopped or
crushed

2 tsp ground coriander

½ tsp ground turmeric

½–1 tsp chili powder

juice of ½ lemon

Indian bread or cooked basmati rice,
to serve

Put the potatoes in a medium saucepan and pour in the hot water. Bring to a boil, then reduce the heat to low and cook, covered, for 6–7 minutes, until the potatoes are al dente. Add the chickpeas and cook, uncovered, for 3–4 minutes, until the potatoes are tender.

Add the coconut milk and salt and bring to a slow simmer.

Meanwhile, heat the oil in a small saucepan over low heat. Add the garlic and cook, stirring frequently, until it begins to brown. Add the coriander, turmeric, and chili powder and cook, stirring, for 25–30 seconds.

Fold the aromatic oil into the potato mixture. Stir in the lemon juice and remove from the heat. Serve immediately with Indian bread or cooked basmati rice.

COOK'S TIP

You can use green beans or a mixture of green beans and carrots instead of the potatoes. Black-eyed peas are also excellent for this recipe.

Black-Eyed Peas & Mushrooms

This is a combination made in heaven—tender black-eyed peas with their earthy, nutty taste combine extremely well with the mildly earthy mushrooms, which absorb the flavors of the spices beautifully. The rich, red tomato sauce with flecks of emerald green mint shows off the creamy peas and mushrooms like a pretty picture.

SERVES 4

1 onion, coarsely chopped

4 large garlic cloves, coarsely chopped

1-inch/2.5-cm piece fresh ginger, coarsely chopped

4 tbsp sunflower oil or olive oil

1 tsp ground cumin

1 tsp ground coriander

½ tsp ground fennel

1 tsp ground turmeric

½–1 tsp chili powder

6 oz/175 g canned chopped tomatoes

14 oz/400 g canned black-eyed peas, drained and rinsed

4 oz/115 g large flat mushrooms, wiped and cut into bite-size pieces

½ tsp salt, or to taste

¾ cup warm water

1 tbsp chopped fresh mint

1 tbsp chopped fresh cilantro leaves

1 small tomato, seeded and cut into julienne strips, to garnish

Indian bread, to serve

Process the onion, garlic, and ginger in a food processor or blender.

Heat the oil in a medium pan over medium–high heat and add the processed ingredients. Cook for 4–5 minutes, then add the cumin, coriander, ground fennel, turmeric, and chili powder. Stir-fry for about 1 minute, then add the tomatoes. Cook until the tomatoes are pulpy and the juice has evaporated.

Add the black-eyed peas, mushrooms, and salt. Stir well and pour in the warm water, then bring to a boil, cover the pan, and reduce the heat to low. Simmer for 8–10 minutes, stirring halfway through.

Stir in the chopped mint and cilantro and remove from the heat. Transfer to a serving dish and garnish with the strips of tomato. Serve as a main course with Indian bread or as an accompaniment to meat, fish, or poultry dishes.

Lentils with Fresh Chiles, Mint & Cilantro

This recipe is characteristic of the cooking of the Punjab in north India; like the people of this state, the cooking is robust, lively, and full of character. Two types of lentil are first sautéed with aromatic spices, then simmered until tender. Traditionally, a type of lentil, known as urad dhal, *which you can buy from Indian stores, is used, but this recipe uses split red lentils as they are more readily available.*

SERVES 4

⅓ cup split red lentils (masoor dhal)

⅓ cup skinless split chickpeas
   (channa dhal)

3 tbsp sunflower oil or olive oil

1 onion, finely chopped

2 tsp garlic paste

2 tsp ginger paste

2–3 fresh green chiles, chopped
   (seeded if you like)

1 tsp ground cumin

2½ cups warm water

1 tsp salt, or to taste

1 tbsp chopped fresh mint

1 tbsp chopped fresh cilantro leaves

¼ cup unsalted butter

1 fresh green chile and 1 small tomato,
   seeded and cut into julienne strips,
   to garnish

Wash both types of lentil together until the water runs clear and let soak for 30 minutes.

Heat the oil in a medium saucepan, preferably nonstick, over medium heat and add the onion, garlic paste, ginger paste, and chiles. Stir-fry the mixture until it begins to brown.

Drain the lentils and add to the onion mixture together with the cumin. Reduce the heat to low and stir-fry for 2–3 minutes, then pour in the warm water. Bring to a boil, reduce the heat to low, cover, and simmer for 25–30 minutes.

Stir in the salt, mint, cilantro, and butter. Stir until the butter has melted, then remove from the heat. Serve garnished with the strips of chile and tomato.

Mixed Lentils with Five-Spice Seasoning

Bengali five-spice seasoning, or panch phoran, *is a typical combination of whole spices used in east and northeast India. As you will see from the ingredients list below, they are all whole spices and are highly aromatic. A winning combination of yellow mung beans and split red lentils (known as* mung dhal *and* masoor dhal*) is used here. The golden lentils, boldly patterned with chopped tomatoes and fresh green cilantro, and dotted with black mustard and nigella seeds, look quite stunning and taste delicious.*

SERVES 4

generous ½ cup split red lentils (masoor dhal)

generous ½ cup skinless split mung beans (mung dhal)

3¾ cups hot water

1 tsp ground turmeric

1 tsp salt, or to taste

1 tbsp lemon juice

2 tbsp sunflower oil or olive oil

¼ tsp black mustard seeds

¼ tsp cumin seeds

¼ tsp nigella seeds

¼ tsp fennel seeds

4–5 fenugreek seeds

2–3 dried red chiles

1 small tomato, seeded and cut into strips, and fresh cilantro sprigs, to garnish

Indian bread, to serve

Mix both types of lentils together and wash until the water runs clear. Put them into a saucepan with the hot water. Bring to a boil, then reduce the heat slightly. Boil for 5–6 minutes, and when the foam subsides, add the turmeric, reduce the heat to low, cover, and cook for 20 minutes. Add the salt and lemon juice and beat the dhal with a wire whisk, adding a little more hot water if the dhal is too thick.

Heat the oil in a small saucepan over medium heat. When hot, but not smoking, add the mustard seeds. As soon as they begin to pop, reduce the heat to low and add the cumin seeds, nigella seeds, fennel seeds, fenugreek seeds, and dried chiles. Let the spices sizzle until the seeds begin to pop and the chiles have blackened. Pour the contents of the pan over the lentils, scraping off all the residue from the bottom of the pan.

Turn off the heat and keep the pan covered until you are ready to serve. Transfer to a serving dish and garnish with tomato strips and cilantro sprigs. Serve as a main course with Indian bread or as an accompaniment to meat, fish, or poultry dishes.

Tarka Dhal

The word tarka means "tempering." Tarka dhal is easy to cook, as the boiled dhal is simply tempered with a few whole spices, and either onion (or in this case shallot) or garlic is added to the hot oil before being folded into the cooked lentils.

SERVES 4

1 cup split red lentils

3½ cups water

1 tsp salt, or to taste

2 tsp sunflower oil or olive oil

½ tsp black or brown mustard seeds

½ tsp cumin seeds

4 shallots, finely chopped

2 fresh green chiles, chopped
   (seeded if you like)

1 tsp ground turmeric

1 tsp ground cumin

1 fresh tomato, chopped

2 tbsp chopped fresh cilantro leaves

Wash the lentils until the water runs clear and put into a medium saucepan. Add the water and bring to a boil. Reduce the heat to medium and skim off the foam. Cook, uncovered, for 10 minutes. Reduce the heat to low, cover, and cook for 45 minutes, stirring occasionally to ensure that the lentils do not stick to the bottom of the pan as they thicken. Stir in the salt.

Meanwhile, heat the oil in a small saucepan over medium heat. When hot, but not smoking, add the mustard seeds, followed by the cumin seeds. Add the shallots and chiles and cook, stirring, for 2–3 minutes, then add the turmeric and ground cumin. Add the tomato and cook, stirring, for 30 seconds.

Fold the shallot mixture into the cooked lentils. Stir in the cilantro, remove from the heat, and serve immediately.

COOK'S TIP

If you add salt too soon to the lentils, they will take longer to cook.

Egg & Lentil Curry

This egg and lentil curry is an excellent source of protein for vegetarians. The lentils soak up the flavors of the spices beautifully. Chapattis make an ideal accompaniment to this dish.

SERVES 4

3 tbsp ghee or vegetable oil

1 large onion, chopped

2 garlic cloves, chopped

1-inch/2.5-cm piece fresh ginger, chopped

½ tsp minced fresh chile or chili powder

1 tsp ground coriander

1 tsp ground cumin

1 tsp paprika

⅓ cup split red lentils

1¾ cups vegetable stock

8 oz/225 g canned chopped tomatoes

6 eggs

½ cup coconut milk

2 tomatoes, cut into wedges

salt

fresh cilantro sprigs, to garnish

chapattis (see page 188), to serve

Melt the ghee in a saucepan, add the onion, and fry gently for 3 minutes. Stir in the garlic, ginger, chile, and spices and cook gently, stirring frequently, for 1 minute. Stir in the lentils, stock, and tomatoes and bring to a boil. Reduce the heat, cover, and let simmer, stirring occasionally, for 30 minutes, until the lentils are tender.

Meanwhile, place the eggs in a saucepan of cold water and bring to a boil. Reduce the heat and let simmer for 10 minutes. Drain and cover immediately with cold water.

Stir the coconut milk into the lentil mixture and season well with salt. Process the mixture in a blender or food processor until smooth. Return to the pan and heat through.

Shell the hard-cooked eggs and cut in half lengthwise. Arrange three halves on each serving plate. Spoon the hot lentil sauce over the eggs, adding enough to flood the plate. Arrange a tomato wedge and a cilantro sprig between each halved egg. Serve hot with chapattis.

Accompaniments

Chapattis

In Indian homes, chapattis are made every day, using a flour known as atta. *Asian stores sell atta, but you can substitute whole wheat bread flour combined with all-purpose flour, at a ratio of two thirds whole wheat to one third all-purpose.*

MAKES 16

scant 3 cups chapatti flour (atta),
    plus extra for dusting

1 tsp salt

½ tsp sugar

2 tbsp sunflower oil or olive oil

generous 1 cup lukewarm water

Mix the chapatti flour, salt, and sugar together in a large bowl. Add the oil and work well into the flour mixture with your fingertips. Gradually add the water, mixing at the same time. When the dough is formed, transfer to a counter, and knead for 4–5 minutes. The dough is ready when all the excess moisture is absorbed by the flour. Alternatively, mix the dough in a food processor. Wrap the dough in plastic wrap and let rest for 30 minutes.

Divide the dough in half, then cut each half into 8 equal-size pieces. Form each piece into a ball and flatten into a round cake. Dust each cake lightly in the flour and roll out to a 6-inch/15-cm round. Keep the remaining cakes covered while you are working on one. The chapattis will cook better when freshly rolled out, so roll out and cook one at a time.

Preheat a heavy-bottom cast-iron grill pan or a large heavy-bottom skillet over medium–high heat. Put a chapatti on the pan and cook for 30 seconds. Using a thin spatula, turn over and cook until bubbles begin to appear on the surface. Turn over again. Press the edges down gently with a clean cloth to encourage the chapatti to puff up—they will not always puff up, but this doesn't matter. Cook until brown patches appear on the underside. Remove from the pan and keep hot by wrapping in a piece of foil lined with paper towels. Repeat with the remaining dough cakes.

Chile-Cilantro Naan

Naan came to India with the ancient Persians, and it means "bread" in their language. Naan is traditionally made in the tandoor (Indian clay oven), but this can be emulated by using a very hot broiler.

MAKES 8

3¼ cups all-purpose flour

2 tsp sugar

1 tsp salt

1 tsp baking powder

1 egg

generous 1 cup milk

2 tbsp sunflower oil or olive oil, plus extra for oiling

2 fresh red chiles, chopped (seeded if you like)

1 cup fresh cilantro leaves, chopped

2 tbsp butter, melted

Sift the flour, sugar, salt, and baking powder together into a large bowl. Whisk the egg and milk together and gradually add to the flour mixture, mixing it with a wooden spoon, until a dough is formed.

Transfer the dough to a counter, make a depression in the center of the dough, and add the oil. Knead for 3–4 minutes, until the oil is absorbed by the flour and you have a smooth and pliable dough. Wrap the dough in plastic wrap and let rest for 1 hour.

Divide the dough into 8 equal-size pieces, form each piece into a ball, and flatten into a thick cake. Cover the dough cakes with plastic wrap and let rest for 10–15 minutes.

Preheat the broiler to high. Line a broiler pan with a piece of foil and brush with oil.

The traditional shape of naan is teardrop, but you can make them any shape you wish. To make the traditional shape, roll each flattened cake into a 5-inch/13-cm round and pull the lower end gently. Carefully roll out again, maintaining the teardrop shape, to about 9 inches/23 cm in diameter. Alternatively, roll the flattened cakes out to 9-inch/23-cm rounds.

Mix the chiles and cilantro together, then divide into 8 equal portions and spread each on the surface of a naan. Press gently so that the mixture sticks to the dough. Transfer a naan to the prepared broiler pan and cook 5 inches/13 cm below the heat source for 1 minute, or until slightly puffed and brown patches appear on the surface. Watch carefully, and as soon as brown spots appear on the surface, turn over and cook the other side for 45–50 seconds, until lightly browned. Remove from the broiler and brush with the melted butter. Wrap in a dish towel while you cook the remaining naans.

Parathas

These are pan-fried unleavened breads for special occasions and religious festivals. Made with lots of melted ghee, parathas have a flaky texture and are too rich for everyday meals—unless, of course, you don't worry about your waistline! For an Indian-style breakfast, try parathas with a bowl of thick yogurt.

MAKES 8

1½ cups whole wheat flour, sifted, plus extra for dusting

½ tsp salt

⅔–¾ cup water

5 oz/140 g ghee, melted

Mix the flour and salt together in a large bowl and make a well in the center. Gradually stir in enough water to make a stiff dough. Turn out the dough onto a lightly floured counter and knead for 10 minutes, or until it is smooth and elastic. Shape the dough into a ball and place it in the cleaned bowl, then cover with a damp dish towel and let rest for 20 minutes.

Divide the dough into 8 equal-size pieces. Lightly flour your hands and roll each piece of dough into a ball. Working with one ball of dough at a time, roll it out on a lightly floured counter until it is a 5-inch/13-cm circle. Brush the top of the dough with about 1½ teaspoons of the melted ghee. Fold the circle in half to make a half-moon shape and brush the top again with melted ghee. Fold the half-moon shape in half again to make a triangle. Press the layers together.

Roll out the triangle on a lightly floured counter into a larger triangle, about 7 inches/18 cm on each side. Flip the dough back and forth between your hands a couple of times, then cover with a damp dish towel. Continue until all the dough is shaped and rolled.

Meanwhile, heat a large ungreased skillet or grill pan over high heat until very hot and a splash of water "dances" when it hits the surface. Place a paratha in the skillet and cook until bubbles appear on the surface.

Use tongs to flip the paratha over and brush the surface with melted ghee. Continue cooking until the bottom is golden brown, then flip the paratha over again and smear with more melted ghee. Use a spatula to press down on the surface of the paratha so it cooks evenly.

Brush with more melted ghee and serve, then repeat with the remaining parathas. Parathas are best served as soon as they come out of the pan, but they can be kept warm wrapped in foil for about 20 minutes.

Pooris

These deep-fried breads puff up to look like balloons when they go into the hot oil, and are perfect for serving with most curries. Children love watching these cooking, but do keep them at a safe distance. Pooris are made in huge quantities to serve at Hindu weddings and special occasions.

MAKES 12

1½ cups whole wheat flour, sifted,
   plus extra for dusting

½ teaspoon salt

2 tbsp ghee, melted

⅓–⅔ cup water

vegetable oil or peanut oil,
   for deep-frying

Put the flour and salt into a bowl and drizzle the ghee over the surface. Gradually stir in the water until a stiff dough forms.

Turn out the dough onto a lightly floured counter and knead for 10 minutes, or until it is smooth and elastic. Shape the dough into a ball and place it in the cleaned bowl, then cover with a damp dish towel and let rest for 20 minutes.

Divide the dough into 12 equal-size pieces and roll each into a ball. Working with one ball of dough at a time, flatten the dough between your palms, then thinly roll it out on a lightly floured counter into a 5-inch/13-cm circle. Continue until all the dough balls are rolled out.

Heat at least 3 inches/7.5 cm oil in a wok, deep-fat fryer, or large skillet until it reaches 350°F/180°C, or until a cube of bread browns in 30 seconds. Drop one poori into the hot fat and deep-fry for about 10 seconds, or until it puffs up. Use two large spoons to flip the poori over and spoon some hot oil over the top.

Use the two spoons to lift the poori from the oil and let any excess oil drip back into the pan. Drain the poori on crumpled paper towels and serve immediately. Continue until all the pooris are cooked, making sure the oil returns to the correct temperature before you add another poori.

COOK'S TIP

To make mini pooris, roll out the dough, then use a lightly greased 1½-inch/4-cm cookie cutter to stamp out smaller circles.

Dosas

In southern India, these ultra-thin, crisp pancakes are served with cilantro chutney or coconut sambal for snacks, or even rolled around a spicy potato mixture and served for breakfast. Dosas are cooked in a thin layer of ghee and therefore have a rich flavor. Remember to start on the batter a day in advance because it needs to soak overnight.

MAKES 8

scant ⅔ cup basmati rice, rinsed

⅓ cup split black lentils (urad dal chilke)

¼ tsp fenugreek seeds

½ cup water

2 tbsp ghee, melted

salt

Bring a saucepan of lightly salted water to a boil, add the rice, and boil for 5 minutes, then drain. Put the rice, lentils, and fenugreek seeds in a bowl with water to cover and let soak overnight.

The next day, strain the rice and lentils, reserving the soaking liquid. Put the rice and lentils in a food processor with 5 tablespoons of the water and process until a smooth, sludgy gray paste forms. Slowly add the remaining water.

Cover the bowl with a dish towel that has been soaked in hot water and wrung out and leave to ferment in a warm place for 5–6 hours, until small bubbles appear all over the surface.

Stir the mixture and add as much extra water as necessary to get the consistency of light cream. Add salt to taste. The amount of salt you need depends on how sour-tasting the batter is.

Heat the flattest, largest skillet you have over high heat until a splash of water "dances" when it hits the surface, then brush the surface with melted ghee. Put a ladleful of batter in the center of the skillet and use the bottom of the ladle to spread it out as thinly as possible, then let cook for 2 minutes, until it is golden brown and crisp on the bottom.

Flip the dosa over and continue cooking for an additional 2 minutes. Turn out of the skillet and keep warm if you are going to wrap around a filling, or let cool. Continue until all the batter has been used.

COOK'S TIP

Don't be tempted to flip a dosa before it has cooked long enough to become crisp on the bottom. It helps to use the largest, flattest pan you have—a skillet or crêpe pan makes the job easier.

Spiced Basmati Rice

This delicately flavored dish comes from Rajasthan and has never fallen from favor since the days of Mogul rule. It is excellent to serve with lamb dishes.

SERVES 4-6

scant 1¼ cups basmati rice

2 tbsp ghee, vegetable oil, or peanut oil

5 green cardamom pods, bruised

5 cloves

2 bay leaves

½ cinnamon stick

1 tsp fennel seeds

½ tsp black mustard seeds

2 cups water

1½ tsp salt

2 tbsp chopped fresh cilantro

pepper

Rinse the basmati rice in several changes of water until the water runs clear, then let soak for 30 minutes. Drain and set aside until ready to cook.

Melt the ghee in a flameproof casserole or a large saucepan with a tight-fitting lid over medium–high heat. Add the spices and stir for 30 seconds. Stir the rice into the casserole so the grains are coated with ghee. Stir in the water and salt and bring to a boil.

Reduce the heat to as low as possible and cover the casserole tightly. Simmer, without lifting the lid, for 8–10 minutes, until the grains are tender and all the liquid is absorbed.

Turn off the heat and use two forks to mix in the cilantro. Adjust the seasoning, if necessary. Re-cover the pan and let stand for 5 minutes.

COOK'S TIP

For spiced saffron basmati rice, lightly toast 1 teaspoon of saffron threads in a dry skillet over medium–high heat until you can smell the aroma, then immediately tip them out of the skillet. Bring the water to a boil while the rice soaks, stir in the saffron threads and the salt, and set aside to infuse. Follow the recipe above, using the saffron-infused water in place of the plain water.

Mint & Cilantro Rice with Toasted Pine Nuts

The slender grains of fragrant basmati rice complement the delicately flavored pine nuts, both prized ingredients from northern India, in this sumptuous pilaf. With its age-old reputation for being rare and costly, saffron adds an exotic touch.

SERVES 4

good pinch of saffron threads, pounded

2 tbsp hot milk

generous 1 cup basmati rice

2 tbsp sunflower oil or olive oil

2-inch/5-cm piece of cinnamon stick, broken in half

4 green cardamom pods, bruised

2 star anise

2 bay leaves

2 cups lukewarm water

3 tbsp fresh cilantro leaves, finely chopped

2 tbsp fresh mint leaves, finely chopped, or 1 tsp dried mint

1 tsp salt, or to taste

scant ¼ cup pine nuts

Soak the saffron in the hot milk and set aside until you are ready to use.

Wash the rice in several changes of cold water until the water runs clear. Let soak in fresh cold water for 20 minutes, then let drain in a colander.

Heat the oil in a medium heavy-bottom saucepan over low heat. Add the cinnamon, cardamom, star anise, and bay leaves and let sizzle gently for 20–25 seconds. Add the rice and stir well to ensure that the grains are coated with the flavored oil.

Add the water, stir once, and bring to a boil. Add the saffron and milk, cilantro, mint, and salt and boil for 2–3 minutes. Cover tightly, reduce the heat to very low, and cook for 7–8 minutes. Turn off the heat and let stand, covered, for 7–8 minutes.

Meanwhile, preheat a small heavy-bottom skillet over medium heat, add the pine nuts, and cook, stirring, until they begin to glisten with their natural oils and are lightly toasted. Alternatively, cook in a foil-covered broiler pan under a preheated medium broiler, turning 2–3 times, until lightly toasted. Transfer to a plate and let cool.

Add half the toasted pine nuts to the rice and fluff up the rice with a fork. Transfer to a serving dish, garnish with the remaining pine nuts, and serve immediately.

Lemon-Laced Basmati Rice

In this much-loved dish from southern India, the snow-white grains of basmati rice are tinged with turmeric and adorned with black mustard seeds. The main flavor here is that of curry leaves, which is the hallmark of southern Indian cuisine.

SERVES 4

generous 1 cup basmati rice

2 tbsp sunflower oil or olive oil

½ tsp black or brown mustard seeds

10–12 curry leaves, preferably fresh

scant ¼ cup cashews

¼ tsp ground turmeric

1 tsp salt, or to taste

2 cups hot water

2 tbsp lemon juice

Wash the rice in several changes of cold water until the water runs clear. Let soak in fresh cold water for 20 minutes, then let drain in a colander.

Heat the oil in a nonstick saucepan over medium heat. When hot, but not smoking, add the mustard seeds, followed by the curry leaves and the cashews.

Stir in the turmeric, quickly followed by the rice and salt. Cook, stirring, for 1 minute, then add the hot water and lemon juice. Stir once, bring to a boil, and boil for 2 minutes. Cover tightly, reduce the heat to very low, and cook for 8 minutes. Turn off the heat and let stand, covered, for 6–7 minutes. Fork through the rice and transfer to a serving dish. Serve immediately.

COOK'S TIP

It is important to let the cooked rice stand to enable the grains to absorb any remaining moisture. Use a metal spoon to transfer the rice to the serving dish, as a wooden spoon will squash the delicate grains.

Coconut Rice

Regarded as the "fruit of the gods," coconut plays a major role not only in southern Indian kitchens, but also in Hindu religious ceremonies, where it can be used to symbolize a full, rich life. Fittingly, this dish is ideal for all special occasions.

SERVES 4-6

scant 1¼ cups basmati rice

2 tbsp mustard oil

2¼ cups coconut cream

1½ tsp salt

Rinse the rice in several changes of water until the water runs clear, then let soak for 30 minutes. Drain and set aside until ready to cook.

Heat the oil in a large skillet or saucepan with a tight-fitting lid over high heat until it smokes. Turn off the heat and let the oil cool completely.

When you are ready to cook, reheat the oil over medium–high heat. Add the rice and stir until all the grains are coated in oil. Add the coconut cream and bring to a boil.

Reduce the heat to as low as possible, stir in the salt, and cover the skillet tightly. Simmer, without lifting the lid, for 8–10 minutes, until the grains are tender and all the liquid has been absorbed.

Turn off the heat and use two forks to mix the rice. Re-cover the pan and let the rice stand for 5 minutes.

COOK'S TIP

The mustard oil is heated and then cooled in order to reduce the pungency of its flavor. If you prefer to use vegetable oil or peanut oil, you can skip this step.

Cucumber Raita

Raita is a generic name for any salad with a spiced yogurt dressing. In the north of India, the yogurt is flavored with roasted crushed cumin seeds and chile, while southern India excels in making a yogurt dressing with a hot oil seasoning.

SERVES 4-5

1 small cucumber

¾ cup plain yogurt

¼ tsp sugar

¼ tsp salt

1 tsp cumin seeds

10–12 black peppercorns

¼ tsp paprika

Peel the cucumber and scoop out the seeds. Cut the flesh into bite-size pieces and set aside.

Put the yogurt in a bowl and beat with a fork until smooth. Add the sugar and salt and mix well.

Preheat a small heavy-bottom saucepan over medium–high heat. When the pan is hot, turn off the heat and add the cumin seeds and peppercorns. Stir for 40–50 seconds, until they release their aroma. Remove from the pan and let cool for 5 minutes, then crush in a mortar with a pestle or on a hard surface with a rolling pin.

Set aside ¼ teaspoon of this mixture and stir the remainder into the yogurt. Add the cucumber and stir to mix.

Transfer the raita to a serving dish and sprinkle with the reserved toasted spices and the paprika.

COOK'S TIP

To add an extra dimension to the taste and texture of the raita, crush ⅓ cup roasted salted peanuts. Mix half into the raita and sprinkle the remainder on top just before serving.

Cilantro Chutney

This is an example of one of the uncooked, fresh-tasting chutneys that are served with every meal or snack throughout the day in Kerala, starting with breakfast. The bright green cilantro, fresh coconut, and chile capture the flavors of the region.

MAKES 8 OZ/225 G

1½ tbsp lemon juice

1½ tbsp water

3 oz/85 g fresh cilantro leaves and stems, coarsely chopped

2 tbsp chopped fresh coconut

1 small shallot, very finely chopped

¼-inch/5-mm piece fresh ginger, chopped

1 fresh green chile, seeded and chopped

½ tsp sugar

½ tsp salt

pinch of pepper

Put the lemon juice and water in a small food processor, add half the cilantro, and process until it is blended and a slushy paste forms. Gradually add the remaining cilantro and process until it is all blended, scraping down the sides of the processor, if necessary.

If you don't have a processor that will cope with this small amount, use a pestle and mortar, adding the cilantro in small amounts.

Add the remaining ingredients and continue processing until blended. Taste and adjust any of the seasonings, if you like. Transfer to a nonmetallic bowl, cover, and chill for up to 3 days before serving.

COOK'S TIP

For a cooling cilantro raita, stir 1¼ cups plain yogurt into the chutney and chill for at least 1 hour. Sprinkle with plenty of chopped fresh cilantro just before serving.

Chile & Onion Chutney

For those who really like spicy hot food, this fresh chutney packs quite a punch. It's hot, zingy, and can bring tears to your eyes if you don't seed the chiles. Gujarati people will include the chile seeds and serve this at all meals, eating it in the summer like a snack with poppadoms or pooris.

MAKES 8 OZ/225 G

1–2 fresh green chiles, finely chopped
   (seeded if you like)
1 small fresh Thai chile, finely chopped
   (seeded if you like)
1 tbsp white wine vinegar or
   cider vinegar
2 onions, finely chopped
2 tbsp fresh lemon juice
1 tbsp sugar
3 tbsp chopped fresh cilantro, mint,
   or parsley, or a combination of herbs
salt
chile flower, to garnish

Put the chiles in a small nonmetallic bowl with the vinegar, stir, and then drain. Return the chiles to the bowl and stir in the onions, lemon juice, sugar, and herbs, then add salt to taste.

Let stand at room temperature or cover and chill for 15 minutes. Garnish with the chile flower before serving the chutney.

COOK'S TIP
To make the chile flower garnish, use a sharp knife to make several cuts lengthwise along the chile, keeping the stem end intact. Put the chile in a bowl of ice water and let stand for 25–30 minutes, or until the cut edges have spread out to form a flower shape.

For a chile and onion raita, stir 1¼ cups plain yogurt into the chutney mixture and chill for at least 1 hour. Stir before serving and sprinkle with fresh herbs.

Coconut Sambal

Coconuts grow in abundance along the gently flowing backwaters of Kerala, and slightly crunchy fresh chutneys like this are served at many meals. Serve this as a snack with poppadoms or use it as an accompaniment to simply cooked fresh seafood.

MAKES 5 OZ/140 G

½ fresh coconut or 1¼ cups dry
    unsweetened coconut

2 fresh green chiles, chopped (seeded if
    you like)

1-inch/2.5-cm piece fresh ginger, peeled
    and finely chopped

4 tbsp chopped fresh cilantro

2 tbsp lemon juice, or to taste

2 shallots, very finely chopped

If you are using a whole coconut, use a hammer and nail to punch a hole in the "eye" of the coconut, then pour out the milk from the inside and reserve. Use the hammer to break the coconut in half, then peel half and chop.

Put the coconut and chiles in a food processor and process for about 30 seconds, until finely chopped. Add the ginger, cilantro, and lemon juice and process again.

If the mixture seems too dry, stir in about 1 tablespoon of coconut milk or water. Stir in the shallots and serve immediately, or cover and chill until required.

COOK'S TIP
This sambal will keep its fresh flavor for up to three days if stored in the refrigerator.

Mango Chutney

This light, spiced chutney is about as far as one can get from the thick, overly sweet mango chutney sold in jars. It adds the sunny flavor of Goa and southern India to any Asian meal.

MAKES 9 OZ/250 G

1 large mango, about 14 oz/400 g, peeled, pitted, and finely chopped

2 tbsp lime juice

1 tbsp vegetable oil or peanut oil

2 shallots, finely chopped

1 garlic clove, finely chopped

2 fresh green chiles, seeded and finely sliced

1 tsp black mustard seeds

1 tsp coriander seeds

5 tbsp grated jaggery or light brown sugar

5 tbsp white wine vinegar

1 tsp salt

pinch of ground ginger

Put the mango in a nonmetallic bowl with the lime juice and set aside.

Heat the oil in a large skillet or pan over medium–high heat. Add the shallots and sauté for 3 minutes. Add the garlic and chiles and stir for an additional 2 minutes, or until the shallots are softened but not browned. Add the mustard seeds and coriander seeds, then stir.

Add the mango to the pan with the jaggery, vinegar, salt, and ginger and stir. Reduce the heat to its lowest setting and simmer for 10 minutes, until the liquid thickens and the mango becomes sticky.

Remove from the heat and let cool completely. Transfer to an airtight container, cover, and chill for three days before using.

COOK'S TIP
This chutney should be stored in the refrigerator and used within a week.

Tamarind Chutney

There isn't any mistaking the fresh, sour taste of tamarind: it adds a distinctive flavor to many dishes, especially those from southern India. More like a sauce than a thick chutney, this sweet-and-sour mixture is essential for serving with samosas and it also goes particularly well with pan-fried fish.

MAKES 9 OZ/250 G

3½ oz/100 g tamarind pulp, chopped

2 cups water

½ fresh Thai chile, or to taste, seeded and chopped

generous ¼ cup light brown sugar, or to taste

½ tsp salt, or to taste

Put the tamarind and water in a heavy-bottom saucepan over high heat and bring to a boil. Reduce the heat to the lowest setting and simmer for 25 minutes, stirring occasionally to break up the tamarind pulp, or until tender.

Tip the tamarind pulp into a strainer and use a wooden spoon to push the pulp into the rinsed-out pan.

Stir in the chile, sugar, and salt and continue simmering for an additional 10 minutes, or until the desired consistency is reached. Let cool slightly, then stir in extra sugar or salt, to taste.

Let cool completely, then cover tightly and chill for up to three days, or freeze.

Lime Pickle

With chunky pieces of lime, mouthwatering spices, and lots of zest, this hot and tangy pickle is the perfect accompaniment to a whole range of Asian dishes.

MAKES 8 OZ/225 G

12 limes, halved and seeded

4 oz/115 g salt

2½ oz/70 g chili powder

1 oz/25 g mustard powder

1 oz/25 g ground fenugreek

1 tbsp ground turmeric

1¼ cups mustard oil

½ oz/15 g yellow mustard seeds, crushed

½ tsp asafetida

Cut each lime half into 4 pieces and pack them into a large sterilized jar, sprinkling over the salt at the same time. Cover and let stand in a warm place for 10–14 days, or until the limes have turned brown and softened.

Mix the chili powder, mustard powder, fenugreek, and turmeric together in a small bowl and add to the jar of limes. Stir to mix, then re-cover and let stand for 2 days.

Transfer the lime mixture to a heatproof bowl. Heat the oil in a heavy-bottom skillet. Add the mustard seeds and asafetida to the skillet and cook, stirring continuously, until the oil is very hot and just starting to smoke.

Pour the oil and spices over the limes and mix well. Cover and let cool. When cool, pack into a sterilized jar. Seal and store in a sunny place for a week before serving.

COOK'S TIP

If you are planning to serve this hot pickle on a particular occasion, it is best to start preparing it a month in advance. Unlike most Indian chutneys, it cannot be eaten immediately after making.

Index

Award-winning writer Mridula Baljekar is a best-selling author of many Indian cookbooks. She was born and raised in northeast India and when she moved to England she turned her childhood passion for cooking into a highly successful career.

Mridula presented her own series, "Mridula's Indian Kitchen," and the highly acclaimed "Spice Trail" on Carlton Food Network in the U.K. In India she appeared on the most popular channel NDTV and also Door Darshan. She is regularly invited to present cooking shows on regional and national radio stations such as LBC Radio, BBC Southern Counties, BBC Berkshire, BBC Birmingham and the Food Programme on Radio 4.

She owned a contemporary Indian restaurant in Windsor, Berkshire, England, which won several prestigious awards. Mridula has now sold her award-winning restaurant in order to concentrate on her writing and media career. As well as running highly successful cooking classes, she is developing a range of chutneys and prepared meals which she hopes to put on the supermarket shelves very soon.

Mridula's food has been described in the media as "Heaven on Earth for the senses," "route to spice heaven," and "traditional Indian cuisine with a brilliant modern twist."

Bibliography
Grove, Colleen and Peter. *Curry Culture*. Menu Publications, 2005
Norman, Jill. *Complete Book of Spices*. Dorling Kindersley, 1990.